Sociology:
The Basics

What is sociology?

Can sociologists change society?

In a subject which has changed greatly in the last twenty years, this book provides an essential introduction to the world of sociology. The author analyses key areas of the subject as well as presenting concise definitions of sociology's major concepts and theories.

Each chapter covers essential areas of study, including the nature of human society, science and sociology, social institutions and the future of sociology. The book also provides suggestions for further reading. Clearly written, comprehensive and informative, *Sociology: The Basics* is an indispensable introduction for anyone thinking of studying the subject.

Martin Albrow has held Chairs of Sociology in Cardiff and Munich and is Visiting Professor at the London School of Economics and in the University of Cambridge. He is Research Professor in the Social Sciences, Roehampton Institute London. His most recent book is *Do Organizations have Feelings?* (Routledge 1997).

Other titles in this series include:

Politics: The Basics
Stephen D. Tansey

Language: The Basics
R.L. Trask

Philosophy: The Basics
Nigel Warburton

Sociology:

The Basics

- Martin Albrow

LONDON AND NEW YORK

First published 1999
by Routledge
11 New Fetter Lane, London
EC4P 4EE

Simultaneously published in the USA
and Canada
by Routledge
29 West 35th Street, New York,
NY 10001

*Routledge is an imprint of the Taylor &
Francis Group*

© 1999 Martin Albrow

Typeset in Times and Frutiga by
The Florence Group, Stoodleigh, Devon
Printed and bound in Great Britain by
Clays Ltd, St Ives plc

*British Library Cataloguing in
Publication Data*
A catalogue record for this book is
available from the British Library

*Library of Congress Cataloging in
Publication Data*
Albrow, Martin.
  Sociology: the basics / Martin Albrow
    p.   cm.
  Includes bibliographical references
and index.
    1. Sociology.   I. Title.
HM1.A625 1999
301–dc21   98–56183
                          CIP

ISBN 0–415–17263–2 (hbk)
ISBN 0–415–17264–0 (pbk)

For the three Woodies, Nick, John and Stephen,
and Thomas A-O

Contents

Preface   xi
Acknowledgements   xiii

1   The nature of human society   1

The world and society   2
From species to humanity   5
   Humankind and culture   5
   Sex and gender   8
   Evolution and history   11
Shaping the world   13
   Money and capital   13
   Institutions and collectivities   17
   Countries and nations   20
   The globe   21
Human society in practice   23
   Social relations   23
   Types of human association   25
   Constructing and performing society 27

2 The science of sociology 31

The rise of the discipline 31
Science and reality 31
Origins 34
Paradigms and discourse 37
Methods of research 41
Theory and metaphor 41
Concepts in research 43
Explanation 46
Triangulation 49
Intellectual craftsmanship 52
Professional practice 56
Ideology and objectivity 56
Freedom for values 59
Professionalism 62
Lifelong learning 65

3 Sociological theory 69

Old and new directions 69
The old theoretical agenda 69
The contemporary problem for theory 72
The unit of analysis 75
Power and critique 77
Constituting society 81
Ideal types 81
Mediation 84
Sociation 90
Structuration 94
Boundaries and identities 99
Difference 99
Identity 101
Trust 103

4 Social institutions 107

From functions to practices 107
Institutions in practice 107

Institutional theory   110
Changes in the life-spheres   114
   Beyond state societies   114
   Work for human needs   119
   Environment as global risk   126
   The autonomy of culture   131
   Persons and God   135
Beyond institutionalism   138

5   Society in the future   141

Open futures   141
   The ignorance society   141
   The control freaks   143
Accounting for change   145
   Surviving the present   145
   Grand narrative   149
The future of capitalism   153
   Capitalist society   153
   The limits of capitalism   155
   Scenarios   159
Towards a human society   163
   Specialisation and reductionism   163
   Precarious humanity   165
   The way ahead   166

Note references   171
Further reading   181
Index   185

Preface

This is a marvellous time for setting out the basics of sociology. Its subject, society, is once again in the limelight after twenty years in the shade. All disciplines go through periods of flux. They advance, even in disarray. But there have to be moments of consolidation.

There have been periodic restatements of the key issues in the discipline since Herbert Spencer wrote *The Study of Sociology* in 1873.[1] They took stock of existing knowledge and argument in the field and provided useful benchmark discussions for their time.[2] My aim is to emulate their approach.

There has been a gap since 1970 when we have had many 'introductions', 'invitations' and arm-stretching textbooks, but only the rare survey of the basics of the discipline. In this time the subject has changed enormously. Now it is an urgent necessity to retie the threads which link us with the classic origins of the discipline.

At the same time we have to redefine the scope of sociology in the light of social transformation. The

main reason for the flux of the subject has been the shift into a new age when West, East, and modernity itself have become dated concepts. Society under global conditions requires us to rethink *its* basics.

This is why society has come back into vogue for politicians. Economics and business studies have shown their limitations in recent years as any academic discipline does if it is expected to answer all the problems for all of the people all the time.

The task for sociology is modest but also vital in a world where there are many essential tasks. Its field of study, human society, is less than humankind, and humankind is less than reality. But if sociology does its work properly we have a better chance to make society fit for a changing world.

This is a non-technical textbook designed to interest the general reader, inform the beginning student and challenge the advanced student. For better or for worse the public expects sociologists to make judgements about society. We have to be confident of ourselves before we can expect public confidence in us.

The past period has been one of sharp disagreement about the scope of the discipline. Sociologists have even disputed the existence of society. The influential journal *The Economist* recently called on them to settle this argument after I aired it at the 1998 meeting of the British Association for the Advancement of Science.[3] This book is a response to that challenge.

Sociology is an essential aid to making intelligent judgements about society's direction in a changing world and our place in it. Given the ever-increasing pace of social transformation this makes it a necessary part of lifelong learning.

The lesson of our own work is that any activity, including science and within it sociology, depends on society. This is the most basic of basics for and from sociology. You can't take society for granted. That's why its study at any level is fraught and fascinating at the same time.

Acknowledgements

Thanks to Lorraine Radford for her account of her research experience, to Darren O'Byrne for his suggestions on Chapter 3, to Jane Elliott and Jane Grubb for reading and making helpful comments on earlier versions, to Susan Owen for her Windows Presentations skills and for successfully putting the theory of family friendly employment into practice.

I am grateful to my colleagues at the Roehampton Institute London, both in and outside the School of Sociology and Social Policy, at the University of Cambridge Faculty of Social and Political Sciences and at the London School of Economics Department of Sociology who have generously supported my theory that social relations are proved through absence, and to Linda Wilson who has unfailingly shown that time and space can be compressed to everyone's satisfaction. Thanks also to Alan Fidler for his careful copy-editing.

Mari Shullaw has made the kind of input to this project which only an experienced Senior Editor can

make and I have been indebted to and grateful for her detailed comments and professionalism at every stage. On this occasion an author is going to pin some responsibility for whatever has gone right on someone else.

Chapter 1

The Nature of
Human Society

Sociology is the study of human society, or societies. But such a simple initial definition of the subject begs the question 'What is human society?' This chapter answers this by setting out its unique properties which make it different from anything else in creation.

The second chapter shows how sociology selects its own range of scientific methods to explore the special nature of human society, with the third chapter setting out the theoretical ideas which have inspired and been developed through this research. The fourth chapter applies sociology to achieve greater understanding of how political, economic or cultural institutions work.

Finally, the fifth chapter draws on sociology to help answer the question of where society might be going. So though the book begins with the nature of society, by the end we have established that in a changing world its nature is always in question.

We study society not because it is fixed, obvious and permanent, but because it is fluid, elusive and

changing. It is this flux which makes living in society a challenge for each of us as individuals. We need to be able to find our bearings in it. This is why sociology, as it charts and documents this shifting basis for our lives, has an ever-renewed fascination.

Ceaseless movement may be daunting but it also offers room for manoeuvre. It means that we can all hope that our lives can make a difference to society however limited our sphere of activities may be. Indeed sociology can help us realise such a hope so far as it sets out the extent and limits of our powers. That's reason enough for writing this short book.

The world and society

There is a difference of emphasis between talking of society in the singular or in the plural. 'Society' in the singular appears more general and unlimited over any time or space, taking in all human beings. The plural, 'societies', sounds more like a set of container units distinct from each other, as if you can take them one by one to inspect their contents.

In fact sociology has always studied societies, both taken separately and also all together, as 'human society'. The balance between the two aspects may vary, but in the end the study of the one absolutely requires study of the other. Neither makes sense on its own.

For instance, consider the United States as a society. We can think of it in cities, factories, schools, farms or prisons. We also find it in what politicians do, in what people see on the media or in what they believe about God. We recognise the connections between these things. We might treat them as confined within the boundaries of the United States and refer to them under the general heading of 'American society'.

But for every link to the territory of the United States there will also be links beyond. People in prison may be there because they have been caught with drugs. But these don't simply arrive out of the blue. People travel across national boundaries to supply them. These are 'connections', the theme of the American Academy Oscar award winning film *The French Connection* where Gene Hackman as the New York cop shows the federal agents how to break a US drug ring. He does it by smashing it abroad – in Marseilles in France.

The film may amount to subtle propaganda to make us see drugs as foreign, un-American and therefore to be resisted. But 'foreign connections' are essential to the most law-abiding institutions. The 'local' church may well also be 'foreign' at the same time. The Roman Catholic Church is a world-wide organisation with headquarters in Rome. The Unification Church began in Korea. The President of the United States discusses shared problems, is 'at home' with leaders of other nation-states. Ford is a global corporation, making and selling cars world-wide. So is Mazda. They both have plants in Detroit.

The boundaries of a country, its people and culture are only maintained through constant interaction with other countries. The great majority of people in the United States can trace their ancestry back to foreign countries. People's ties to countries are not natural facts, even though they may fix them to land. Boundaries and nationality have to be made and then 'recognised', and then they are always subject to change.

Where is the Soviet Union now? Where are Soviet citizens? The term 'international relations' has customarily been used for political relations between nation-states. But relations between countries are social as well as political, and, for that matter, economic and cultural too.

Yet societies are both more and less than countries. While we often call a country a 'society', we can use that word for a collection of any number of people whose activities link them in some way. We thus refer to the Mafia, the Freemasons, Rotary as societies. Nothing stops us using it for Amnesty International, the Green Movement, or equally McDonald's if we recognise that even the most single-minded profit-making business depends on the people who control and work for it.

In all these cases relations across state boundaries are as much part of the maintenance of the society as connections within. Indeed societies are always potentially transnational, whether they be state inspired or voluntary, religious or economic. So where does that leave 'countries'? It's better to refer to them as 'human collectivities' and return to this point later.

Clear-cut boundaries do not make society any more real. Societies extend over time and space and it's often difficult to say where they begin and end. Some societies endure for millennia, as the Chinese or Christian, others less than a century like the Soviet Union. Some have spread over the globe, like capitalist society has done since the sixteenth century, while others are very localised and ephemeral, like the Brotherhood of Independent Workers which lasted in Cleveland from 1942 to 1944.[1]

We can date the beginning of the Brotherhood with a meeting of 50 workers in the Thompson Main engineering plant in 1942. It faded out in 1944. It was small and local, began and ended. But like any society its reality was a thread woven into the lives of people. Its existence did not rest just on their occasional co-presence in a meeting room but in mutual dependencies on which they based their activities when they were apart.

Neither society in general nor societies have to be attached to a particular patch of earth. Countries are often called 'nation-state societies' and it is their special feature that they lay claim to territory. But family and friendship are vital aspects of society. They are not normally tied to a place, or indeed a particular time. Nor are corporations or churches.

Only recently have we reinstated the idea that societies are not essentially tied to territories. In the eighteenth century the Scottish professor Adam Ferguson (1723–1816) observed that modern people had come to think of the loss of land as the end of society whereas the ancient Greeks laughed at their enemies as they escaped a conquered city.[2] Four centuries earlier the great Arab judge and sociologist before sociology, Ibn Khaldun (1332–1406), wrote a treatise on how societies change and was in no doubt that they were essentially mobile and held together by the human spirit.[3]

The physical limit of any society is the earth, which is also the medium for its movement. When we put down roots at any spot we create our own world which is why we can't equate 'world' and 'earth'. So when we talk about societies, in the plural, moving in a 'world', this varies for each, is a construct, a heritage of special links with an environment which is both a human achievement as well as a set of natural conditions.

If we add up all these special worlds we have a sum of worlds which is far larger than the earth can bear. It is within this larger world of worlds that we find human society. Because societies traverse the earth, expanding and contracting, they are bound constantly to cross and recross each other. Their fates depend on their ongoing relations with each other, especially as these centre on their respective share of the earth and its resources. They can relate through conflict or mutual aid, competition or alliance. The outcome of these struggles is a collective fate for humankind as a whole.

From species to humanity

Humankind and culture

Human society in general, not just societies in the plural, extends to all human beings, the total number of members of the animal species, *homo sapiens*. But we should not equate the human species with human society. As with other animals the qualities of the species are distributed among individual members. In total they make up humankind. It is through their social relations that they constitute societies and the total set of relations at any one time makes up what we can call world society.

For any animal species the essential requirements for survival include genetic inheritance, functioning organisms, a favourable environment and social relations. Society as such is not especially human. If we take our closest animal relatives, chimpanzees, in their natural habitat in Africa they constantly form and reform social relations, fission–fusion male-dominated societies, within larger territorially based exclusive communities. In captivity female coalitions develop to reduce male dominance. But both in the wild and captivity chimpanzees exhibit a diversity and adaptability in their social behaviour which permits wide variation in prevalent social relations.[4]

It is this adaptability which human beings possess too which makes it impossible to show that any particular type of society is determined by biology. Individuals during their lives are capable of sustaining and experimenting with vastly differing types of social relations. Societies can undergo total social transformation as the history of revolutions shows.

In evolutionary terms the human organism has not just adapted, it has evolved adaptability. It provides for versatility, a collective freedom to draw on a vast repertoire of possible social behaviours under differing conditions. The range of social relations which human behaviour can support extends from individual freedom of choice to arbitrary rule of some over others. Hence the variations in human society are vast even while the biology remains stable, and explaining the sources of these variations is a distinct field of inquiry in its own right.

What makes human society a special case compared with the societies of other species is the development of culture, ways of acting, thinking and feeling which are transmitted from generation to generation and across societies through learning, not through inheritance. Culture includes language and technology both of which involve the communication of ideas and the possibility of sophisticated co-ordination of action. This vastly enhances adaptability.

It is not that other animals do not possess culture. Chimpanzee groups exhibit learning and the transmission of culture over time in the group. But the culture of human societies everywhere has been so much more developed for so long that it may have exercised an evolutionary influence on the human organism. This is what Edward Wilson calls gene–culture coevolution.[5] Culture confers selective advantages for the organism with the larger brain, specialised larynx and prolonged period of maturation to adulthood which have evolved in the period of perhaps five or six million years since we shared a common ancestor with the chimpanzees.

But there is no evidence that the recent incremental development of culture since historical records began has required biological change. It has depended on increases in the scale and intensity of human social relations which it also helps to promote. Culture provides the repertoire of activities from which we choose and creates the resources we need to pursue them. It is both a product of collective effort and a means for individual expression. Language has both those features, but so also have art, science, education, religion and sport. We are able to perceive their abstract qualities as values.

Human efforts are channelled by values in certain directions and the outcomes of those efforts are in turn evaluated and become the basis for future efforts. This reflexive relation between values, activities and products absorbs and directs the energies of human beings. It is the basis of the transformation of nature and the environment for which archaeology provides the earliest evidence and which historically is ever accelerating. These are collective achievements which make possible the accentuation of individual difference. This is one of the more important paradoxes we and governments often find puzzling. Individualisation, as self-realisation and political project, depends on quite definite arrangements for sharing in a collective product.

Culture depends on individuals for continuous dismantling, reassembling and modification, but even more on social relations and the larger configurations of those relations we call societies. Society then has a quite definite place within the order of our world – set between species and culture, and an environment which in part we have made, it is our relations with each other, providing both a base and limits to what we as individuals can do.

In respect of society culture is a double-edged acquisition. Based on social relations it can also transform them. It provides guides and criteria which people take account of in their daily behaviour. These are norms which are always ambivalent; that is, they become facts in so far as we follow them but are ideals when we fail to measure up to them. The regulation of our behaviour by standards which we can choose to obey or not is a core feature of the human condition.

To culture we owe humanity, standards for our behaviour and the values we aspire to in a truly human existence. Yet it can equally produce inhumanity, the application of technology in genocidal horrors like the Holocaust. This was the most dramatic deformation of culture which the developing technology of the Modern Age produced. But that was merely a horrific episode in a period of recent history.

Now we are on the threshold of a transformation of the species, a possible new evolutionary stage when the potential exists not just to destroy people but to change genetic inheritance. The new genetics is important because it opens the possibility for science to change the biological basis of human life even as it fails to show that society is determined by genes. The 50–100,000 genes in the human genotype provide the preconditions for culture not its direction. This is provided by an alliance between scientific values and capitalistic interests, taking us into uncharted territory.

Sex and gender

The interplay of biology, society and culture always arouses the most intense controversy in discussions of sex, sexuality and gender. There are radically diverse views about the differences between the sexes, but also about what is typical, expected or appropriate in their relations with each other.

The intensity of debate arises in part from the complexity of the issues. The influences on each other of society, culture and human biology are not one way, nor straightforward. For instance the biological nature of human beings itself provides for social relations, and the topic of sex and gender is a main point of entry into understanding society.

Biologically human beings are built to reproduce themselves through relations with each other – namely, those social relations we call sexual. Changes in reproductive potential can influence society. For instance if, as some evidence suggests, males world-wide are losing fertility, perhaps for environmental reasons, this might mean declining demand on women's capacity to bear children. In turn this might enhance the freedom of women in their relations with men.

But this is a long causal chain with many links. Male fertility is arguably the least important factor in determining the number of children a woman has, and relations between men and women are the outcome of politics and economics as much as of sex. There are plenty of other ways women may be subordinated to men quite apart from child-bearing.

The importance of sex for society is not simply as a reproductive mechanism but as a primary differentiation between individuals which creates mutual dependencies between them. Sexual identity is global in two senses. It applies to everyone. In market researchers' terms it is a global category. Second, it travels world-wide, meaning that you carry this attribute wherever you go. In this sense the fact of being male or female crosses the boundaries of any society and is testimony to the unity of the human species. A sexual identity, being male or female, will be ascribed to you from birth, whether you want it or not, irrespective of sexual orientation, heterosexual or homosexual.

Relations between men and women are never exempt from considerations based on sexual difference. A central issue for any society is how far those concerns should go. Societies vary vastly in the extent to which they define activities and social positions as appropriate for each or just one sex. These varying definitions of the characteristics and proper behaviour for men and women are what we refer to as gender, those signs which people use to convey differences in sexual identity. We read male/female difference into a vast range of everyday things, in looks, work, clothes and language. But those signs vary from culture to culture, within and across societies.

The case of language makes us aware that the gender difference need not have anything directly to do with sex at all. In a language like French every noun reflects the gender difference. The sun, 'le soleil' is masculine in French, 'die Sonne' feminine in German, but the world as a whole is gendered in any culture even if not directly represented in grammar. In Chinese culture the male and female principles pervade the world and are represented by the mystical yin–yang sign which now is recognised world-wide. But this entwined embryonic globe interpreting the forces of life vividly illustrates that cultural expression of gender is only remotely determined by underlying sexual differences. Human beings give free play to their imagination and creative power in the expression of gender and variations in that expression exist between and within both societies and individuals.

At the same time gender competes with other principles as an organising factor in social life and is often concealed to serve other purposes. In particular power relations are gendered so that men worldwide have almost always enjoyed the greater share of the benefits of wealth and had easier access to public position and employment. Patriarchy, male rule, can persist while disavowing itself. Thus in the contemporary capitalist world business interests often seek to impose principles of rationality, efficiency and competitiveness and exclude questions of gender from work organisation. This appears to be consistent with political demands for 'equal opportunities', but it may effectively entrench male domination. Mary Wollstonecraft who made the classic nineteenth-century affirmation of the rights of woman sought to persuade them to 'endeavour to acquire strength too'.[6] Rights have to be asserted as generations of feminists have sought to do ever since. Removing gender from the agenda does not produce equality any more than equality before the law in the market has redistributed wealth.

The refusal to recognise the consequences of gender difference does not make it go away. Nor does legislation abolish sexuality. Sexuality is a social force, as well as a property of individual organisms. As a force for shaping social relations it extends vastly further than biological reproduction. It can bond couples of the same sex. But sexuality belongs no more to separate couples than it does to separate individuals. It pervades the whole of social life.

This means we can't marginalise sexuality as something outside society. Indeed it is a prototypical medium for all social relations. It belongs to individuals by virtue of their prior relations with others. It appears as energy which can be converted to different forms. It is lodged in objects, fetishised. It can be promoted and exploited commercially. It contributes to the climate of organisations.[7] It is maintained over time in and through relations with other people.

The channelling of that force is a potent factor in the formation of social relations. For instance, human beings in general avoid sexual relations with those with whom they have close relations in early life. This is backed up by culture, by the incest taboo, but it appears also as an emotional response which may have a biological basis. One obvious interpretation is that it prevents the genetic defects which arise out of inbreeding.[8] But this avoidance occurs whether the individuals are biologically related or not. For instance, children of the same Israeli kibbutz do not marry each other even though they are not related biologically and there is no taboo.

A more plausible interpretation is that sexual avoidance among close associates in early life encourages sexual search beyond them and thus promotes relations between social groups, increasing the scope and power of alliances between communities. If there has been evolutionary selection of an innate response it may then be the result of the superior survival chances of larger groups.

Sexuality as input, medium and outcome is then tied into the total configuration of social relations. As society changes so does sexual behaviour. In the past periods of free sexual expression have alternated with periods of restraint. Liberalising political regimes, relaxed social control, and sexual permissiveness were linked in Europe in the 1900s and the 1960s. What the psychoanalytic theory of Sigmund Freud and the erotic painting of Gustav Klimt did for middle classes in the earlier period was repeated for a mass market by the Rolling Stones and Carnaby Street (aided by the contraceptive pill) in the later.

When we refer in this way to the cultural expressions of sexuality it is evident that they cross the boundaries of groups and societies, easily transgressing their established norms of appropriate sexual behaviour. A woman born and brought up in Bangladesh but moving to the West finds the general expectation that she should move around openly in public an uncomfortable and embarrassing exposure. Conversely a Western woman walking on the streets of Dacca with bare arms will invite contempt. At the same time culture is constantly challenged by and changing through these encounters.

Human beings are caught between their universal acceptance that male and female are different sexes and a seemingly limitless variation in cultural expression of difference. This is the tension between sex and gender, between a biological divide and its cultural definition, which has always to be resolved in actual social relations.

Evolution and history

We tell the story of changes in culture and society as human history in the broadest sense; what has appropriately been called grand narrative. This collective self-awareness is itself a feature of culture. It enables us to distinguish different time-lines in our accounts of the species, its individual members, culture and society. Putting them together reflects the extraordinary diversity of actual life. Separating them makes for clear analysis and permits us to develop theories about their interplay.

In particular, maintaining different time-lines for culture, society and the species guards against major fallacies which beset thinking about the human past. We won't fall into the trap of thinking that individuals today are more intelligent, creative, or caring than they were 10,000 years ago. They simply live under quite different conditions. We can guard too, if we think in terms of animal species, against treating social virtues as peculiarly human.

This will help too to forestall the idea that the development of culture, especially of a technical kind, where one invention builds on the last, marks the progress of society from savagery to barbarism and civilisation. This was the dominant belief in the West in the nineteenth century. We can distance ourselves too from the notion that societies have to go through necessary stages of development until they achieve the state of being fully 'modern'. This reflected dominant Western ideology in the twentieth century.

The sheer pace and diversity of changes in culture only highlight the relative independence of social relations. Very different alternative arrangements are possible at the same time in the same society. In the United States today patriarchy persiqts in fundamentalist Christian families and egalitarianism in politically correct liberal couples. Or similar collective organisation may occur at very different periods of history – direct democracy for instance in ancient Greece, among native Americans before the United States was formed, or in service clubs or co-operatives today.

It makes some sense to talk of the development of culture in terms of building on past achievements, which is what the nineteenth century meant by increasing civilisation. But with society on the other hand there is a continual process of dismantling and reconstruction. This is why there is no clear direction in its evolution. Different social arrangements have different survival value, depending on the historical circumstances.

Overall, for human society as a whole we may be able to say that the development of culture has made it possible to sustain far more complex networks of social relations, but when we take any particular society then its future course is always open. The fate of business organisations is instructive here. Large size in itself never guarantees success or survival, and the case for any particular pattern of social relations, say centralisation versus decentralisation, is always contingent on circumstances.

Human society is neither in a permanent steady state nor advancing inevitably. If either were true it would not be half so interesting. It both resists and succumbs to cultural change, it bears utopian hopes and apocalyptic fears, it is subjected to collective experiment or worshipped as divine creation.

Sometimes human society is likened to a well-functioning system, but it is more like a ramshackle edifice in constant need of maintenance and repair. It also repeatedly requires reconstructions as human beings increase in numbers, now approaching six billion, on the same size plot of land since they first appeared on earth. Our recent awareness of the global risks to humankind should encourage new efforts towards world-wide co-operation. If we succeed it will be the triumph of hope over experience.

Shaping the world

For each one of us, making a living means inhabiting a world we have not made and of which we can only seek to shape a minute part. Our societies too are embedded in complex engagements with the environment, which human beings before us have shaped. Our social relations are bonded into entities where the moving or visible parts are bodies, machines, buildings, commodities, images, and texts. These often conceal as much as reveal those very relations on which they depend. In a world of objects we forget the child labour in the fine Eastern carpet, or the community severed by the oil pipeline.

But our collective engagements with the world and our construction of an environment are the essential setting for any account of our social relations. These are summations of past culture, the capacities of the species as well as social relations. They are the actuality of human experience, the changes of which are recorded as history and for which we have to render an account before we can consider the specific nature of human society.

Money and capital

In the course of human history, apart from the advance of science and technology, the most pervasive change which has taken place in the relations of culture and society is the development of money. Because each one of us needs it to live we tend to forget its significance in the wider account.

In cultural terms money is the most influential and widely used measure of values. It enables us to compare objects and activities by their price or market value. Where people work for money a monetary value can also be put on things which are not bought and sold. We can put a price on leisure by calculating lost income from not working. Even though religious values are not bought or sold we can ask how much people will sacrifice to observe them. We can compare different types of food with each other, food with clothes, consumer goods with housing, or social services with military expenditure. Most importantly for production we can compare the costs of raw materials, labour and capital with the returns from sales.

Market value is one thing, what each person regards as true value is another. Each person seeks uniquely to realise their own values and find true worth regardless often of what other people think or what market values are. Nearly everyone has possessions they would never dream of selling. They might give up everything for the sake of faith or love of another person.

We also resist trade-offs between values like health, liberty, truth and courage which appear unique and incomparable. Who can say whether health is worth more than education? People often resent money measures in these areas, which is why so many countries have social provision for them. For while money provides recognisable measures of value we may still not accept the validity of the implicit order of values which prices suggest. These are determined not by some democratic poll of the value judgements of members of society, but by wealth, effective purchasing power, which is distributed very unequally.

The expenditure of those with most money will have a dominating influence on the hierarchy of values in any market. The sociologist and economist Thorstein Veblen (1857–1929) pointed out that money was often spent simply on 'conspicuous consumption', showing others that you were wealthy.[9] Expenditure demonstrated high status.

But to make that expenditure requires disposable income which is normally acquired from wealth, the control of resources which can generate money income. In other words, behind the apparent objectivity and precision of money measures of values lurk power and society. In modern society this social power came to take the form of capital.

In its origin the idea of capital, which has been taken up in 'capitalism', referred to money which was put to use as a loan as distinct from the interest on that loan. So it hinted at all those other uses of the term 'capital' where it means what comes first, is more important, leads or is at the head, as in 'capital city'. This notion of capital was pleasingly clear-cut. It was only in the eighteenth century that economists began to extend it to take in not just financial resources but any wealth which could be used to generate future wealth. This was at the time when leaders of states were looking to the new science of political economy to tell them how to create more wealth. One historian of economics has complained:

> What a mass of confused, futile and downright silly controversies it would have saved us, if economists had the sense to stick to those monetary and accounting meanings of the term instead of trying to deepen them.[10]

But of course the political economists were seeking the secrets of why money was worth something and recognised that money itself only had value in relation to the uses to which it was put, to what it bought, or to what went to make the things which were bought. In any case the idea behind capital, even in its original financial sense, was of value which could be the basis for future values; taking it beyond money to things which could be bought was only an extension of the underlying idea.

So given the transformation of the Industrial Revolution in Europe by the middle of the nineteenth century it seemed obvious to Karl Marx that capital, beyond finance, above all else meant the productive powers of modern industry, which were owned by the newly named 'capitalists'. Marx wrote of the capitalist system and not of capitalist society. It was for him 'bourgeois', reflecting the city origins of the new class of factory owners. But he declared a vital link between society and capital, for factories were worthless without labour. Capital therefore was the social relation of capitalists and workers. What the one owned depended on the work of the other; that work depended on the capital of the first.

In fact capital has grown in ways Marx did not envisage and beyond any simple opposition of capitalists and workers. Financial capital is as important as industrial capital and much of this represents the savings of pension funds and insurance companies. Intellectual property, ownership of rights in inventions, films, books, computing software are a form of cultural capital increasingly important in contemporary society. So too are the trained capacities of people in specialised occupations which require long periods of preparatory study. This is human capital. This is all in addition to capital in the form of land or buildings and to social capital, the institutions which provide the infrastructure of social order, community organisation and reliability in social relations on which future value depends.

This diversification of types of capital has taken place with changes in its ownership. While wealth is still overwhelmingly concentrated in a few hands in Western societies, the state is the largest employer, and large proportions of the population have sufficient capital in the form of housing and pension entitlements to remove any interest they might have in revolution, the threat with which Marx alarmed the ruling classes for almost a century.

The confrontation of owners and workers in the workplace is no longer the focal social relation in contemporary society. The key relation is between service providers and consumers in which each transaction is a measurable contribution (even if negative) to capital, however it is distributed. Those relations are then exposed to global change to the extent that capital itself has a global unity.

There is now a widespread understanding that the organisation of capital is profoundly important for the shaping of social relations generally between people who have no direct contact with each other. This is why we talk of capitalist society. But this is only a special case of the money relation where exchanges take place on the basis of confidence in the soundness of money and trust in the people who use it. Mismanaged money, as in Germany in the 1920s, can wreak havoc and destabilise society. Without the massive inflation of those years the Nazis might never have come to power.

A well-managed currency converts easily into any other currency. In this way it means that the transaction between any one customer and a shopkeeper is only one moment in a chain of relations which may cross the world. With the communications of the late twentieth century, the buyer and seller, producer and consumer can be any distance apart on the globe. Money binds us all into one world economy and at the same time frees us from dependence on any one producer or purchaser. As such it is a force for individualisation and globalisation at one and the same time.

The main problem for society is that the popular trust in money which makes it viable as a world-wide means of exchange and measure of value seems also to involve acquiescence in a concentration of capital, which allows overwhelming influence on values to be exerted by a few people and especially by corporations. For example the world-wide popular concern for the environment under conditions of global warming is currently thwarted by the power of energy corporations. A few collectivities can impose an agenda which institutions are not powerful enough to resist.

Institutions and collectivities

The independence of money from personal control, its widespread acceptance, its continuity beyond your life and mine, the way it penetrates other aspects of human existence, the need for its management and technical control are not unique to it. Rather they make it an example of one of the most important general features of human society: the social institution.

Money as an institution shows too how relations between people are concealed behind calculations of the abstract qualities of material things. In general, institutions embed social relations in material things and technology, in life-spheres – which in the case of money we call 'the economy'. Institutions are sequences of social practices which are widespread, impersonal, subject to, and yet always resistant to control.

What is true for money and the economy applies equally to life-spheres like law, education, science, religion, sport, medicine, art, government – with institutions like litigation, examining, experiments, communion, competition, consultation, exhibitions and elections. Each is maintained in and through social relations even as each constrains, shapes and facilitates our lives.

In the contemporary world the life-spheres in which institutions are embedded become fields for specialist practitioners on whom we all depend: bankers, lawyers, teachers, and so on. Equally, no matter how specialised the activities which develop in any one sphere, they involve participation on the part of a much wider group of people than just the specialists.

The grounding of institutions in people's relations provides sociology with one of its most important tasks in the contemporary world. It explores the way institutions are based in social relations and lodged in the wider society, not excepting, indeed especially including, those spheres like law, science, medicine and the economy which often appear to have been taken over exclusively by the experts. This will be the special subject of Chapter 4.

For the moment we need to note the way institutions involve cultural definitions of social relations as they incorporate values and techniques in practices. The main concern of institutions is the definition of right practices irrespective of the people involved. But they never escape, however much they strain at, the bonds of human association.

Everything that is done in society is done by people. This is true of institutions and applies to all projects, whether massive, like the exploration of space, or rather minor, like painting my house. They are explained not by reference to the personal characteristics of the people involved but by the general logic of human practices in relation to the world.

Practices are shaped in customs, conventions, usages, rituals, styles, manners, fashions, tastes, plans, projects, procedures, laws, as well as, of course, institutions. They are lodged in the world such that people relate to each other in certain material settings and with practical ends in mind. The boundaries around these are often bonds between people. Working means both belonging to a firm and going to a factory. Learning is both a matter of belonging to a class of pupils and attending a school.

Sometimes the boundaries in a physical and social sense coincide so closely that the activities are exclusively conducted by one group of people behind walls, as with a prison, barracks or asylum. Erving Goffman (1922–82) drew our attention to these by calling them 'total institutions' and also to the fact that so much social activity takes place in 'establishments' of one kind or another where we allude ambiguously at the same time to technology, people or setting.[11]

Very often the building itself becomes the name of the institution – the church, university or office. We can never be sure at first whether the talk is about a building, people, or set of practices. Goffman calls his total institutions 'hybrids', part community, part organisation. Bruno Latour says all these mixes of society and nature, 'collectives' in his terms, are 'hybrids' and the examples he gives include even a nuclear power plant and the hole in the ozone layer.[12] This provocative formulation calls on us to recognise the intimate connections between nature and society.

We both make and organise around material things. Consider the car. We often hear about 'the impact of the car'. But no producers, no car. No drivers, no impact. When driven the car is a human/machine unity and in this way it is a factor in making our world. Similarly we talk of the 'household'. The house with its people is the purchasing unit which makes sense for market researchers. It is in and through the household that its members consume and spend. There is no need to talk here about 'the family'.

But what holds these hybrid objects together? Human beings of course mainly, though in diverse ways, and I call them *human* collectivities for that reason. The bonds which tie them together and make them objects for our concern, however, remain open to inquiry. In particular the social relations embedded in them are often obscure. In any one household we don't even know in principle how many people belong to it, let alone how they relate to each other. These are all open questions, with answers depending on the facts of the case.

With both institutions and collectivities we know that social relations are central to them and that they could not exist without them, but they are never inscribed on the surface. Society makes our worlds possible, enables us to fulfil our needs and spin our fantasies. But we have to search for its reality in our experience of the world. This is especially true for countries.

Countries and nations

In everyday usage people often talk about 'America', 'Britain', or 'Germany' as 'societies'. But our discussion of human collectivities must make us pause for thought. On a map these may be labels for land areas depending on when and where it was made. 'America' may be a continent, or two, or a political unit. Is 'Britain' just an island? Where was 'Germany' before it became one country in 1870, or between 1945 and 1989 when it was two?

Even commonsensically we have to know something to be able to use these terms competently. The terms 'Americans', 'the British', 'Germans' are no less ambiguous. Do they refer to citizens of a nation-state or to those sharing in a culture? After all German-speaking people could include Austrian and some Swiss people. 'Americans' might refer to people outside the United States, while 'British' can even refer to people who have no right to come to live in the United Kingdom.

Nothing becomes clearer by referring to American, British and German 'society' or 'culture'. Reference to language does not help. The German language may convey German culture, but the Americans and British scarcely share English culture because they speak English. If one talks of 'the global power of US culture' it sounds like the Americanisation of the world, except that it is the consumer requirements of the world market rather than of the United States which dictate to Hollywood. Replace Americanisation by 'globalisation' and United States culture is under threat.

What then are countries? We should distinguish at least four facets:

1 *Nation:* the sum of people who share a nationality.
2 *Culture:* ways of acting, thinking and feeling which can be learned.
3 *State:* institutions which enforce a public good.
4 *Territory:* a land, sea or air area.

These are very different things which often do not coincide but which we throw together when we speak of America or Germany doing something. It is often at this point that *society* is introduced. In other words when you link state, territory, nation and culture you get society.

So both in everyday usage and among modern sociologists terms like 'South Africa', 'Kenya', 'Chile' etc. are often used for countries or societies without making any distinction between them. 'Society' then appears to be the term which cements our experience of the intimate connections between territory, state, culture and nation.

However the term 'country' or 'land' is perhaps more expressive of these ties. Moreover these are nation-states too, which means we should sort out the connections between nation and society. If we do we will find that nation-states are only one special version of society.

In fact some have come to the conclusion that the names applied to countries have no very clear meaning and no necessary reference to society. A celebrated sociologist, Norbert Elias (1897–1990) called these names 'verbal symbols of a collective entity with numinous qualities'.[13] Historians can be equally sceptical. The great historian of world civilisations, Arnold Toynbee (1889–1975) called names like France 'mythological proper persons' and not nearer to reality than 'Marianne' or the 'Gallic cock'.[14] In these terms 'United States' and 'Uncle Sam' are equally ambiguous.

We don't have to be so sceptical. The reason these names loom so large is that they do provide a continuity in the stories people tell each other and in tales of the human past. They refer to complex entities in which state, culture, territory or nation are bonded in varying untidy ways which do not have neatly coinciding boundaries. In this sense countries are a particular kind of human collectivity. They are more than just societies, but, as with any collectivity, social relations are crucial for their maintenance.

Countries, or in earlier times and even now, 'peoples' when they are detached from territory, are the subjects of humanity's big story, and have been ever since the earliest accounts. Society has an important place in this story, but it is not the whole tale and has a lesser role than the largest collectivity of all – humankind.

The globe

In a series of stages in the twentieth century a new collective consciousness has arisen where the globe, rather than national territories, appears as the arena in which the fate of the human species and society will be determined. The concerns of the early twentieth century were dominated by the idea of class conflict producing a crisis of social order. In mid-century the frame for understanding the human condition was very much set by nation-states projecting their solutions to internal conflicts as world-wide recipes.

But these ideas of conflict within society prepared the way for a global vision. We only need an external shock to recognise that implied in the oppositions of us and them, men and women, capitalists and workers, there is a larger unity. We understand that these are relations which variously divide and unite people wherever they are. This is the message of the Palestinian Edward Said who has pointed out that 'the East' is an age-old construction of the West in its bid to control the whole world.[15] 'West' and 'East' imply each other and cannot exist apart.

Numerous shocks in the late twentieth century, from the threatened nuclear apocalypse after the Hiroshima nuclear bomb in 1945 through to the collapse of the Soviet empire and the recognition of the threat of global warming, have brought a sense of a collective fate in relation to the globe as a whole. With global awareness these structural oppositions in society cede primacy to a concern for our collective relations with the environment.

Once we consider all human beings as belonging to one great society there are no outsiders. For much of this century sociologists followed the dictum of Émile Durkheim (1855–1917), the founder of French professional sociology, who sought to explain the social solely by the social.[16] But when we consider the globe as a whole plainly the physical conditions of human existence have an intricate influence on the shape of society. In the late twentieth century world-wide public concern seeks to shape society to accord with sustainable development even as economic growth seems to run out of control. These are contradictions within all our lives rather than a conflict between 'them' and 'us'.

The German sociologist Ulrich Beck calls this contemporary condition 'risk society', where we calculate opportunities and threats to ourselves in a world which we do not control.[17] This alerts us to the break from an earlier period of history, the Modern Age, when the progress of human society was considered as a continuous expansion of human control, over nature and over society itself.

This was very much a reflection of the outlook and interests of nation-states as they sought to shape society to the needs of the international system of the nineteenth and early twentieth centuries. Then, nation-state, country and society were taken to mean the same thing. When the question of the relation of individual and society was addressed it was treated as a problem of how the nation-state could ensure the commitment of its citizens to its requirements.

'Socialisation' once meant the raising and education of children to become adult members of the nation-state. Now education means the constant process of enhancing the capacities of people to play an independent and responsible part in shaping a world where they choose among societies. Citizenship in the Global Age measures nation-states by the needs of humankind.[18]

Human society in practice

Social relations

We have to identify the concept which corresponds to a world of shifting boundaries and changing collectivities. It needs to express both the erection and dismantling of barriers and to leave open the possibility of the transformation of social entities in the course of human activities. We find it in the idea of social relations.

No matter how vast the society – for instance Asian or even world society; or separate, perhaps a ghetto; or focused, say, for the protection of birds; or general, as with 'the family' – social relations are involved. Indeed, we can see all these societies or groups as different ways in which relations between people take shape and persist over time in a recognisable form. The idea of social relations conveys the vast variability and potential range of human society and societies without prejudging their unity, the boundaries between them, or their duration.

We have social relations with enemies as much as with friends. We may interact with people half way round the globe as much as with our next-door neighbour. We can relate to previous or coming generations, even if they can no longer, or cannot yet, respond.

23

The Englishman Herbert Spencer (1820-1903), who more than anyone else popularised sociology world-wide in the nineteenth century, gave this illustration of connectedness over space and time: 'A derangement of your digestion goes back for its cause to the bungling management in a vineyard on the Rhine several years ago.'[19]

He conveys how important the organisation of social relations is in its consequences for people's lived experience. They may not realise this, nor want it either. Society does not happen just as people wish it. It often confronts them as a fact. Equally people may also often try to blame someone else for something they could have avoided. Spencer plausibly illustrates how far-off social causes can make you sick. But does his choice of example unintentionally reveal British xenophobia? Is he blaming the consequences of a heavy night on the 'Huns'?

We can then go further than the definition of sociology in the first sentence of this chapter. It may also be defined as the study of *people in their social relations*. When we talk about 'societies' in the plural we have in mind the ways social relations both unite and divide people. The divisions between the British and the Germans, for instance, are displayed *within* their relations with each other.

So relations between people may constitute a business firm, but its existence depends also on their relations with other people, like customers, suppliers, or even competitor firms. Its rivals relate to it in the special system of relations known as a market, where they may not know each other personally but still find themselves constrained by unknown others.

All types of human groups or associations from families to nation-states depend equally on internal and external social relations. In a school, relations internal to it, between teachers and pupils especially, depend on relations outside it, with parents, examination authorities, funding agencies and the state. Put another way, families cross the boundaries of schools; are both in them and outside them.

Human social relations are always incomplete in the sense that they always have to be renewed through what people do. They are none the less real for that. In the last twenty years purely mathematical work on rational choice has shown that it is advantageous for individuals to recognise pre-existing social relations. Indeed the idea that society might arise as a result of individuals, independently of existing social relations, agreeing to establish them through a social contract, is a fiction from an old modern time.[20] Social relations, and this has been part of a longer tradition of common wisdom about society, are not under the control of the parties to them. With computer simulations in our time social scientists can show that alliances and coalitions have properties of their own which the parties to them ignore at their own cost.[21]

Types of human association

It is through seeing how human associations like families cross the boundaries of collectivities and relate to institutions that we recognise how groups persist independently of material conditions and circumstances.

There was a time when sociology was much concerned with the general classification of groups and institutions, setting out the major types of association as, say, primary and secondary, and then communal as opposed to organisational and then, again, dividing institutions into those of, say, control and communication.

But the distinction between institution and association is one of emphasis. One can either begin the study of society with certain people and asking what they do, or with certain practices and asking who engages in them.

However, except in the limiting, non-existing case of a completely closed society, in which everyone behaves the same way, the two approaches never come to the same point. Behaviour is diversified within groups and also crosses group boundaries. This is why the notion of social relation is prior to that of the group.

Membership and participation never come to the same thing. Not everyone attending the football game is a member of the club; not every club member attends. The ideal of solidarity is utopian, but also in an important sense anti-social, for how else could groups relate to and survive in the wider society except by being internally diverse and open.

We will take this issue up again in Chapter 3. For the moment, though, let us just note that, going back into prehistory, societies have been open, and the almost universal taboo on incest is the guarantee that for the vast majority of people groups must always link with other groups. Society is made up of groups or associations of all kinds, from couples, partnerships, queues, teams, networks, clubs, crowds, communities, parties, cliques, organisations, corporations, nations, movements, even to societies.

When we see such lists of groups the thing which strikes us at once is their diversity – not just in size but also in their claims on their members, in their durability and in their 'groupness', how tightly and exclusively they are organised. We even ask whether a crowd or a movement is a group at all; surely they are too fluid some might say. Is it not the football supporters who make the group, and the crowd is just the result of what they do, coming together on a certain occasion?

There are a number of issues here. One is the feeling that perhaps we should reserve the word 'group' for human beings who have a kind of touching, feeling relationship of an intimate kind. But even in the most intimate relationships people spend most of their time not actually touching and a lot of the time out of each other's presence. Just as a social relationship does not depend on continuous presence of the parties to it, neither does the existence of a group depend on its members sharing a single place.

Even so we may still feel that the questions of fluidity and boundaries are such that it is difficult to talk of, say, the Green movement as a 'group'. Surely movement means just that, people moving, and this is a question more of people doing things rather than merely belonging. In fact movements like the Greens or the Feminist or the International Workingmen's Movement of the nineteenth century are closer to what we have called institutions rather than groups. Indeed movements are one of the ways in which people explore the relationship between doing and being in social life.

Whether you are regarded as member of the Green movement may be a matter of other people judging your behaviour in aiding the recycling of household waste. Whether the Green movement exists depends on the social relations of those who recycle. The constant shifts between being and doing are at their most prominent with social movements, but they characterise social life in general. The membership of groups is as much a question of construction as is the building in which a group meets.

But as with buildings the constructed character of a group does not mean it is any less real. Groups may change more rapidly than buildings, but speed is as real as stability. For good or bad, deeds are real in their course and their effects.

A great deal of sociology is concerned to document and explain the special reality of human groups and practices in their constantly changing manifestations. The scope of this concern can extend from the rise and fall of a civilisation over centuries, to the origins and course of a riot over a few hours.

Constructing and performing society

We have already identified 'relations between people' as necessary to the idea of human society. We talked of them as durable, widespread, and resistant to control. We implied that these features in themselves allow us to talk about society as a fact of life.

The idea of society rests on relations between people and brings us to recognise entities which are configurations of those relations. These are simultaneously outcomes of human action which come and go and never take a final determinate shape. Society contains both social entities and their flux.

We may get a bit frustrated by these constant shifts between objects and processes, between people and things. One moment we are talking about society as a fixed object; at another moment about forming and reforming society through human practices.

For example, one of the important changes since 1945 in Western countries has been the growing acceptance of different kinds of sexual relationships. If our main concern as a sociologist is to fit these to a predetermined classification of married versus non-married, and to pigeon-hole people accordingly, we may miss what is most interesting – namely, to explain just what meaning people give to marriage and sexuality today and how they come to make or not make partnerships of all kinds. To do that we are bound to take people's own accounts seriously and 'the family' in a traditional sense may not figure in them.

27

It is difficult to find adequate language to capture the flux of society, but that is because, like any reality, society is more than just the language we use to account for it, and natural language has its limitations. Everyday language tends to separate objects from processes, certainly from actions. In the sentence 'Jo bakes a loaf', 'Jo' is a person, the verb 'bakes' refers to the skilful activity, and the noun 'loaf' to the resulting object.

The syntax has the lucid banality of the child's learning to read a book. If we talk about society in the same way we are easily misled. In 'We make a society', 'we' are already society, and society is already in the making. We can hardly say 'Society societies a society', but that is closer to the reality.

For a huge misapprehension results from thinking that just because people can be subjects and human society an object of a sentence, then somehow they can just make it as they want, or alternatively that it has some 'loaf'-like object character. 'Society' is as much in verbs as in nouns. It's all those things that go on between subject and object, and when we study 'it' we also study the deeds, events, changes and processes which are involved in social relations. These relations are neither iron girders nor idle imaginings, they are the ordering and reordering of people's activities with regard to each other.

The concept of society involves the making of society through society. So long as there are people it never stops. It involves continuous making and remaking. It reproduces itself but never stays the same. It depends on people. It is the constantly changing nature and qualities of their relations with each other.

Social relations exist in and through construction and performance which are modes of their special reality. They underlie outcomes, artefacts, collectivities. They are intangible, but always around, never directly visible but always leaving traces. Just incidentally they also provide sociologists with their field of research.

This chapter has stressed the fluidity of society and at the same time the need to render an account which fits the changing times. A snapshot freezes movement however fast, which is what we do with graphic representation. We have a heightened awareness now of society which does not correspond with older nation-state definitions. We

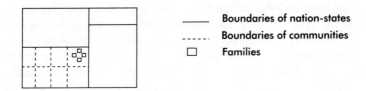

FIGURE 1.1   The imaginary world of nation-state societies

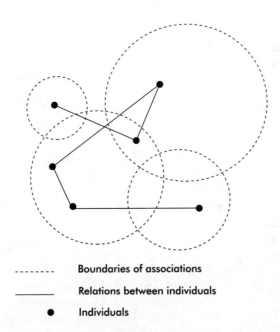

FIGURE 1.2   The imaginary global space of human association

might represent the contrast in two diagrams. The first (Figure 1.1) is the image of a world of nation-state societies, enclosing families in a series of evermore inclusive territorial communities, which abut on to each other without intervening space. The second image (Figure 1.2) is of societies, all kinds of associations which as spheres overlap and interlock, and where individuals cross boundaries and voids as often as they stay within them.

These are visual aids to the imagination. They suggest alternative maps for the territories of society. As possibilities they are one version of the imaginary limits to society which we seek to explore through research into the realities of social relations.

Chapter 2

The Science
of Sociology

The rise of the discipline

Science and reality

To research the reality of society we have to distinguish it from reality in general. Sociology is a serious academic subject, a special science in the sense of a disciplined inquiry. It doesn't span life, reality, the world, the present, but focuses on something much more limited – society.

Society limited! Yes, this is one of the main points of tension between sociology and the ongoing public discussion of society. In everyday language society is ill-defined and barely distinguishable from all those other terms we use to express our feelings about our lives today. Hold-all terms like 'reality', 'states of affairs', 'our life and times', 'the present age', 'the contemporary world' are unavoidable expressions in our conversations, writing and speeches.

We need always to have a way of referring to the wider reality even as we focus on some specific aspect

of it. This is true for academic subjects too. I can't think of doing sociology unless it makes a contribution to understanding the world in which we live. But note it is *only* a particular specialised contribution, not the whole understanding.

'Society' serves at one time as a rallying point, at another as a hate object for conservatives and radicals alike. Sometimes it appears that society is everything human today. Then sociology as the study of society appears to have nothing outside its scope. But a science looks to bring precision, clarity and a defined research agenda to inform what would otherwise be just daily chatter. How can sociology do that if society is the 'world' or 'reality'? There can be no science of reality, though there are many different sciences which reveal specific truths about real things. (There can of course be a specialised study of *concepts* of reality, which is a different matter, and usually identified as philosophy.)

Every science can sin by claiming to explain too much of reality. The early nineteenth-century advocates of sociology Auguste Comte and Herbert Spencer claimed it was the science which made sense of all the other sciences. This made it popular with the general public and rightly unpopular with the rest of the academic world in equal measure.

In the twentieth century the same ambition crops up in another guise. Too many use the phrase 'social construction of reality' as if reality were a human product instead of something which we struggle to cope with and understand. When we add this to a famous injunction 'explain the social by the social' nothing appears to lie outside society or the scope of sociology. Today's hostile critics of sociology call this the Standard Social Science Model, but it isn't standard. 'Sociologism' is an older and better term for exaggerated claims for sociological explanation.

Sociology aims to bring intellectual order to a topic which has got ramifications which extend into our daily lives and into the way governments and professions work. Society is relevant to the work of almost every other discipline. But sociologists prove their worth not by claiming the whole world as their own but by demonstrating special knowledge of that part of reality which is society.

There is nothing about the nature of human society which makes sociologists indispensable. But then that's true for doctors or philosophers with their subject matter. Scientific disciplines don't thrive just because they deal with fundamental things. Bodies, mind and society always have an existence regardless of medicine, philosophy or sociology. People can get by with everyday knowledge of these things. Whether a discipline develops depends on special conditions, like some people having the chance to specialise or to acquire secrets, some showing better than average understanding as a result, others wanting to benefit from that knowledge.

No matter how universal the topic no one is bound to study it. Even if they want to there may be obstacles, like the young Alvy's mother in Woody Allen's film *Annie Hall* who hauled him to the psychiatrist because of his concern for the expanding universe. 'What's that got to do with you?' she yelled at him. Arguably society is almost as important to us as the universe, yet its study often provokes similar hostility, as from parents who mistakenly fear that intellectual interest and moral concern will cut their child off from a rewarding occupation!

Neither the topic in itself nor theories around it can create a discipline on their own. There were plenty of theories about society before sociology, some – like Plato's scheme for the perfect society – profound enough to exercise influence to this day.[1] Sociology isn't alone in having an interest in society. Historians, biologists, psychologists, and economists refer to it all the time. The thing about sociology, as opposed to the other disciplines, is that it makes human society its central concern, not just something incidental. But then that means it crosses the boundaries of other disciplines.

There has been a discussion since its beginning whether sociology is a special discipline or a general one integrating others. In fact the discussion arises for any new discipline. In taking a topic which crosses the boundaries of other disciplines it is at the same time specialised and bonds the others. So genetics crosses the boundaries of chemistry and biology; policy science crosses economics and politics.

Some disciplines like logic have been established long ago, others like media studies are very recent. They arise out of a changing world, changes of interest in it, and the available resources. Sociology has made its own contribution to understanding how disciplines arise,

33

by looking at changing student demand for instance.[2] This kind of inquiry is often called the sociology of science, but that doesn't make the sciences a product of sociology. An understanding of the social conditions for science as an activity helps scientists generally, but it doesn't do their science for them, nor can it purport to do so. But even the most modest sociological research into the social basis of another discipline can arouse surprising hostility.

Origins

Only when a set of research practices and exchange of ideas and results among members of an organised occupation begin to take place can we talk of the arrival of sociology as a discipline. So the invention of the word 'sociology' in 1839 by the French philosopher Auguste Comte (1798–1857)[3] was only a preliminary first step, though his idea that there was a law of three stages governing the development of society became widely known.

Herbert Spencer, a railway engineer from Derby, England, was even more successful as a publicist. His visit to the United States in 1882, travelling by rail, the new revolutionary means of transport, gelled with the American fervour for social improvement, popular education and philanthropy, and the 'sociological movement' took root in colleges and universities. William Graham Sumner, who had given the first lecture course in the subject in Yale University in 1876 addressed a farewell banquet to Spencer saying 'we look upon his work in sociology as a grand step in the history of science'.[4]

By 1895, Albion Small (1854–1926), the founding editor of what is to this day the top general journal of the profession, the *American Journal of Sociology*, was confident enough to write: 'Sociology has a foremost place in the thought of modern [people]. Approve it or deplore the fact at pleasure we cannot escape it.'[5]

By the outbreak of the Great War of the Western nation-states in 1914 the international exchange of ideas and the interest of the state ensured that there were professorships of sociology in most of the great capital cities of the world. National associations for sociology had been founded in the major countries. Governments and voluntary associations were promoting the systematic collection of data on social problems.

The same stimuli promoted the disciplines of statistics, psychology and economics whose development at the time was intertwined with sociology, even as each sought to take charge of a special sphere of interest of its own. This was the time when the social sciences each began to provide an occupational identity and a potential career. Sociology became a subject to study in universities and then in high schools and colleges.

Human society has been around a long time and the ancient Greeks were notable for a developed interest in it. But only in the twentieth century has its study become the dominant concern of a distinct mass higher-education subject. Society has not only been transformed, it has become problematical for individuals, organisations and governments. That's why they are interested in its study.

This historical overview of the origins of sociology itself depends on the sociology of occupations, education and science. 'Sociologies of . . .' fill textbooks and provide special courses for any occupation. For instance the sociology of medicine, social work or law are particularly in demand. These professions all involve direct services to people, and training for them makes explicit recognition of the relevance of sociology.

Each such special field of sociology relates the practices of the occupational area to the wider society and to the social relations of all who deal with it. So the sociology of medicine concerns itself with the social origins of the doctors and paramedical professions, with their social status, their professional ideology, their power in general and over patients, their relations with science and other professions.

Repeatedly sociology shows that an occupation takes a direction which depends as much on social forces as on its values, technical knowledge or even simple demand for its services. But that applies to sociology too. The discipline gets its identity from the special interest people have in society.

This waxes and wanes, possibly being greater in periods of permissive social control (see p. 11). Society then has greater autonomy from the state while the economy is led by consumption for personal social purposes rather than by investment or welfare spending. Business then also has an incentive to undertake research into lifestyles. A lot of market research is sociology under another name.

However, even in centralised and authoritarian regimes the state is also a customer for sociology. For if the aim is to control society, the threat of force is not necessarily the only or best means to secure this. Even the Nazi government of Germany in the 1930s sponsored social research. The controllers want good policy-relevant information and tend to treat the social sciences merely as means to that end; but knowledge can never serve one interest only.

Thus one of the classic topics for sociological research has been social class. The reason it has been so researched in relation to politics and voting behaviour stems from the nineteenth century when the ruling elite in Western nation-states was haunted by the theoretical possibility that the class of industrial workers would take power from them.

This was not an unreasonable fear. The ruling classes were intimidated by the theory of Karl Marx, who predicted the overthrow of a society divided between capitalist and working classes. Later when the working classes everywhere obtained the vote interest turned to the relation between class and voting behaviour. Workers' parties could, and after all, on occasion, as in Britain in 1945, did come to power in democratic states.

So the sociology of politics and of voting became a twentieth-century growth industry. For a time class became the dominant research topic for sociology. It came indeed to be part of almost every explanation of any human behaviour, not just of voting but also of eating, feeling, thinking and speaking. Class as explanation was not just a Marxist interest arising in the 1960s, as many have thought, but pervaded sociology generally.

This concern to determine the importance of class in social behaviour was financed by powerful interests. Political parties wanted to know, but so too did business firms. Their thinking was straightforward. Even if the working class could not overthrow capitalism, if behaviour were linked closely to class membership, then it might be possible to predict which people would buy what goods. Consumption became 'purchasing behaviour'. Public opinion polling and market research were united in their interest in class, and the same organisations developed both activities.

At the very least both commercial and party interests felt the need to know what the main social classes were and how many people belonged to them. In this they shared in an overriding interest of nation-state governments. For tax raising purposes they needed to know how many people there were and where they lived. For their political fate they needed to know who they were. Everywhere in the West the census of the population came not just to record where people lived but also information which allowed them to be assigned to a class, however that was defined.

As early as 1867, when Karl Marx published his account of *Capital*, he could cite a sixfold increase of slaves in the United States between 1790 and 1861 from census returns and he could regroup the statistics of the 1861 census of England and Wales to show how increases in new industrial occupations were accompanied by the growth of an 'unproductive' servant class.[6]

Putting these motive forces together: the state interest in counting people (which, as a specialised study, came to be known as demography); the radical interest in raising consciousness; the commercial interest in identifying social trends; those with a distinctively intellectual interest in understanding society found plenty of willing partners.

But what this account illustrates is that the forces which combine to create an intellectual discipline are not independent of historical circumstances. They are not simply a matter of an intellectual impulse. Nor is the way we talk and think about the time independent of power. The discourse about society by powerful agents within it, like the state or business, contributes to its ongoing formation.

Paradigms and discourse

When Comte devised his programme for sociology he shared the widespread attitude of his time that sciences like physics had shown the way for all knowledge. This outlook is known to this day as positivism after 'the positive philosophy' which is how he described his own work. 'Positivism' refers to any approach which emphasises 'hard' data, predictive theory, and the exclusion of values from research. It treats the natural sciences as providing the model for social science.[7]

But while sociology has drawn lessons from the theories and methods of various natural sciences, it finds that human society has features which require different approaches. The two main reasons are the fact that human society works through culture and because human beings experience themselves and others not as objects but subjects.

It is for these reasons that sociologists argue that the natural sciences, as human products, are embedded in society and culture. Scientists need to bear those limits in mind even while at work in their laboratories. In fact it is a physicist, Thomas Kuhn, who has provided important support for this view with his theory of scientific paradigms.[8]

Kuhn's paradigm is a complex entity, including not simply the topics of science but also theories, methods of research, journals, laboratories, applications, training, rewards and honours and all of these at once. They reinforce each other and when we refer to 'physics', 'economics' or 'linguistics' we allude to the whole range of social practices as well as the theories on which they depend.

The paradigm is then 'normal', what is broadly accepted as constituting the science, and this makes it very difficult to change without something pretty revolutionary, like Einstein's theory of relativity or Crick and Watson's discovery of DNA. Instead of steady progress there are then periods of consolidation, followed by overthrow.

Society is built into this theory of science, indeed the theory draws on sociology which obviously is why it appeals to sociologists.[9] It is not positivistic because it acknowledges that a whole range of factors influence scientific outcomes and directions quite apart from pure ideas or the nature of a world external to the scientist.

The history of science is not one of a simple quest for truth, but of theories and methods which are developed and discarded for a variety of different reasons. For instance, the announcement of a discovery is a media event and often reflects professional rivalry and commercial pressures as much as new truth.

If this applies to science in general then we have to draw its lessons for sociology. Which is what we have done up to now in stressing that, however clear-cut society is as the topic, it is our and other people's interests which direct our attention to it.

The theory of the paradigm suggests we can best approach sociology as a set of practices, including methods of research, organisation, sponsors, training and so on, rather than just theory. Actually sociology is more led by theory than, say, psychology, geography or biology, mainly because there is such a long Western tradition of thinking about society going back to the ancient Greeks.

Sociologists, like any other professionals, including physicians, work through social networks covering the globe, sharing ideas and information in their specialities, 'invisible colleges'.[10] They also work in teams and on collaborative projects, going out to gather data, to observe, record and work in a variety of ways which I will describe a bit later.

But it is a century of research and systematic collection of data which has changed a speculative field into a set of disciplined inquiries which now constitute core understandings of the limits and possibilities of personal, organisational and political projects. There is now no part of thinking about society untouched by sociology.

Sociology finds many ways to express continuing and partly self-induced change in our world. Awareness of this is the most important overall change in the discipline in the last 30 years. We express this in the idea of reflexivity, which is no more than the knower's application of knowledge to change the knower. The most general way this awareness is evident is in the current widespread assimilation of the idea of discourse in sociology.

Discourse is the ongoing exchange and production of ideas in human interaction. It takes place in talk, writing and through any means of communication. It never stops and there is no limit in principle to the numbers who can engage in it. The problem is who takes part. The two major theorists of discourse in the late twentieth century are the German Jürgen Habermas and the Frenchman Michel Foucault. In Habermas's view discourse implicitly has norms of equality and freedom built into it. We can only build full and free communication on the basis of allowing each person the same chance for self-expression in a relationship. On the other hand Foucault asserts that the terms of discourse are always established through power. The very way we talk about sex for instance creates sexuality as male dominance and its definitions and prohibitions actually create objects of desire. This isn't personal to an individual or even to a couple, but part of a process of social construction which is an ongoing discourse with innumerable participants.

This puts power at the centre of sociological analysis; the power to define situations. But this is not in the hands of any one person, any more than a language is determined by the person who speaks it. To speak it is to share in the power it gives. Foucault's people are spokespersons for power more than they are individuals making independent moral choices.

Recognising the importance of discourse in social relations puts severe limits on the scope of positivism in sociology for it brings people's accounts of themselves and the accounts of authorities of all kinds into the frame of research. There aren't just facts, there are the facts of accounts of facts, and so on.

These accounts are not just in words. They are often in numbers too. Numerical counts, statistics, are just as important in shaping our view of the world, and both business and the state devote resources to collecting them and, even more importantly, in defining what is to be counted. These accounts don't just describe the world, they help to make it what it is. Sociology of course collects its own statistics, but much of the time it engages in the use and critique of officially gathered data.

One feature of accounts which has become very prominent in recent years is narrative, the telling of a story as a sequence of events. This is frequently what makes sense of situations for the participants. It applies at a biographical level, but also for collectivities. National history becomes a matter of 'narrating the nation', producing a collective memory which itself defines what the nation is.

Governments are as aware of this as historians or sociologists, and as a result Ministries of Heritage are constructed to preserve a past. Effectively this means that the past as commemorated in monuments and records is continually reconstructed. Sociologists try to detach themselves from this. They are not from their professional training spokespersons for nations or organisations, nor are they outside discourse and narrative. In their own accounts they tell a story of society which has its influence on those who listen.

Methods of research

Theory and metaphor

No research can work without theory, even when it denies it has any. For theory simply means the connection of ideas. Even counting is theory. It requires us to connect ideas of unity, identity, repetition and sequence, which is why it takes some time to learn.

Occasionally people write research reports and claim they contain no theory. This could mean that they are incredibly naive, but normally it signals a rejection of a particular kind of theory. They want to let the reporting and writing and making sense of the world, the 'natural attitude', confront some preconceived set of ideas.

Both quantitative and qualitative research in sociology have their advocates of this kind of approach. One version argues that what emerges is 'grounded theory'. This challenges theories which base accounts of society on ideas of system, structure, market, rational choice, coding or some other frame of thinking drawn usually from other disciplines.

The point is that the theories of other disciplines reflect their concerns with the particular aspect of reality they study. Applied to society they immediately become metaphors or analogies. As one early critic of this approach said, 'social theorists, instead of finding and employing a method and a terminology proper to their subject, . . . on the analogy of the physical sciences they have striven to analyse Society as a mechanism, on the analogy of biology they have insisted on regarding it as an organism'.[11]

Mechanism is not a metaphor in engineering and organism is not a metaphor for the body in biology. The market is not a metaphor for the economy in economics, nor is code a metaphor for language in linguistics. In each case the theoretical idea is a powerful method for analysing the reality. Grounded theory in sociology, even just fact gathering, often called empiricism, has a point if it challenges undue reliance on the metaphorical use of theory from other disciplines.

At the same time if anyone thinks that sociology can proceed without theorising, seeking a deeper understanding of society through developing the ideas connected with its own special reality, then they will progress no further with its study. This means we have to get beyond the metaphors which inhabit everyday discourse too.

For instance, likening a society to a play has long held a grip on the imagination of both playwrights (Shakespeare's 'All the world's a stage') and sociologists. The most famous sociologist in the world in the mid-twentieth century was Talcott Parsons whose theory of society was based on the idea that people fit into roles. The sociologist, who was also the best writer in the discipline, Erving Goffman, employed the drama metaphor, but with focus on the performance rather than the script. There's a lot of scope for acting skill in his *Presentation of Self in Everyday Life*, but we still have to match up to demanding outside requirements if we are going to put on a competent show.

The drama metaphor draws attention to the constraints which society exercises over individual people and the way it proceeds in relative independence from them. This in spite of the fact that it can't work without them. No actors, no performance tonight. But then, on the other hand, no play, no actors. Society is not simply external constraint, it provides opportunities which otherwise would not exist.

We emphasise these features of society when we look at it from the standpoint of individual people. It is external to me and to you, and to every other individual. The stage play, Agatha Christie's *Mousetrap* has been showing continuously in London's West End now for over forty years. No one from the original cast of actors remains and the play goes on.

Just as the play can only be performed by actors so society only exists in what people do. It is then both external and internal. It is constraining but also enabling. So we get nearer to the reality of society if we think of a play in which we make up the parts as we go along. But we can't do it just as we like. 'Theatre', then, is as much a metaphor for the reality of society as 'system', 'organism', or 'market'.

The ease with which we fall into metaphorical discourse shows how elusive is the reality of society. Erving Goffman's emphasis on performance comes close to capturing that reality.[12] But it is not because the idea of performance is imported from drama. That confuses metaphor with reality. Those who can perform on a stage do so because they have *first* learned to perform in life, not the other way round, even if contemporary culture gives us plenty of examples of life become theatre. We have to look for our theoretical concepts in the idea of society itself.

Concepts in research

Sociologists share with philosophers an interest in the meaning of terms, in concepts, and especially the meaning of society, the social, social relations and interaction. But they take that interest beyond just thinking about them. They use them in their research into society.

Go to any textbook and you can find a set of general terms for different varieties of social relations and associations. Standard terms will include community, class, organisation, primary group, kinship group, ethnic group, status group, crowd, movement, audience.

We can readily see that these are not neat pigeon holes. They cross boundaries, merge into each other. We can try to provide fixed meanings for terms like 'community' or 'class' but social reality never seems to correspond exactly to those meanings and they provide unlimited ammunition for controversy.

For instance, people and politicians make loss and rebuilding community one of their main themes. But these days we all experience the babel of voices about what that involves. Some might argue it involves building a 'community centre', others might say that real community needs no centre, some would argue that communities need boundaries and walls, others reject them as artificial intrusions.

Sociologists get involved in this kind of debate, but their contribution is often misunderstood. In the first place they try to 'get real', by exploring the living past and present of communities as aspects of people's experience of social relations and by depicting the vast variety of community-like arrangements – villages and monasteries, refugee camps and company towns, ghettos, slums and fraternities.

They also analyse and identify recurring features in these arrangements, like a sense of belonging, security and familiarity, like-mindedness, shared symbols and norms of behaviour, ordering of status and prestige, periodic celebrations. The strength of these will vary from community to community and they are not exclusive to community either, but any community will display most or all of them.

Then the sociologist will conceptualise, provide a clear-cut image of community, often by developing an idea of community, which will highlight the features which make it different from other kinds of social arrangement, from, say, class or ethnic group. Regularly this concept will be crystallised in a verbal definition. We might define community for instance as 'an enduring set of relations between people based in mutual understandings and shared milieux' and then go on to mention also some of 'belonging, security, familiarity . . .'

Such a definition helps to fix a clear concept. It is not the real thing however. For a start, any community you or I have ever known has not only got mutual understanding, it also has a fair amount of misunderstanding and just plain ill-will. That's often a reason for people to leave it and the world is full of those who have moved to escape communities of one kind or another.

Yet you won't find sociologists redefining community as 'close relations based in ill-will and misunderstanding'. The reason is that real communities actually work also to an idea of community where positive value is placed on trust and mutual support. So our socio-logical definition reflects that reality without endorsing it. We will return to this vital refusal to endorse later.

What we have just described is a three-phase cycle – explo-ration, analysis and conceptualisation. Each phase is a vital part of sociology, but any one without the other two can be partial and misleading. Only with the completion of the three phases do we achieve one of the most widespread and powerful sociological proce-dures. It is also crucial to recognise that we can start with any one of the phases and proceed in any order.

Let's repeat the procedure with another type of society, this time 'class'. This is famously linked with the name of Karl Marx because he based his whole theory of history and the eventual collapse of capitalism on it. But class as idea and experience was well known before him and is still current independently of him to this day. It's part of sociology and everyday language.

We can begin with analysis and examine features of class as identified by sociologists and others, including popular notions. These will include positions of individuals and groups in the economy, the divisions between those who have work, have no work, or don't need to work, the difference between those who control and benefit from economic decision making and those who are controlled by it, the array of life-chances and privileges which go with economic advantages. We can go on to consider how far class involves consciousness of a shared fate with others and what factors lead to that.

We can then turn to conceptualisation, seek to crystallise our idea of class so that it can guide our subsequent explorations. Here we may find that not all the features we have just considered fit neatly together. There are famous disputes about this with class. Perhaps most famous of all is the one where Max Weber differs from Marx by emphasising individual chances in economic markets rather than ownership of the means of production. Perhaps we have to content ourselves with different concepts of class, or we might try to develop an overarching concept with a definition like 'a sub-set of social positions in a system of economic relations'. If we go on to point out that a person's class is the position they share with others which is dependent on economic processes then we have an idea which Marx and Weber share.

However, when we go on to explore class in the real world, guided by our analysis and our concept, we find that we identify a multitude of differences between classes in apparently similar positions. If we take 'peasants', for instance, there are huge differences between the ancient serfs, medieval villeins, Egyptian fellahin, South American gauchos, Soviet collective farmers.

Those realities can take us back to our analysis and our concept of class and lead us to re-examine them. Not only can we enter our cycle of conceptualisation, analysis and exploration at any point, we find that it is endlessly repeatable and always open to revision. Sociology is essentially an open-ended subject.

This open-endedness often gives rise to misunderstanding and we should look at it more closely. For a start it has a much closer engagement with popular ideas than most academic subjects. Each point in our knowledge cycle has an everyday equivalent. When sociologists explore social reality they adopt all kinds of methods for gathering data, including surveys, interviews, searching documents and records, and just travelling and being in the society they study. But we all go to different places and meet different people.

Sociologists analyse their information, theorise about it, calculate and make lists. So do we all. They spend a great deal of time arguing about definitions and these are equally the stuff of everyday debate. Who hasn't engaged in the argument about whether class exists and what it means? Sometimes we are even persuaded to think and see things in another way. This is the 'reflexivity' we have mentioned earlier (p. 39) which is built into human society.

Explanation

Theories require concepts and research depends on both. But the research aims to solve problems and in science the most general problem is explaining why the world is as it is, why it has changed, or how it is likely to change. The timespan of these changes can vary from micro-seconds to millennia. For sociologists, then, the scope of explanation may vary between contributing to explanations of the rise and decline of civilisations at one extreme to the outbreak of a riot at the other.

Note 'contributing', because no science can ignore the fact that the explanation of real world phenomena requires interdisciplinary collaboration. Social relations never exist in isolation, even though they are the focus of sociological explanation. Sociologists can't ignore biology or economics, but the converse applies also. The demand for explanations may arise for all kinds of reason, sometimes out of a desire to intervene and control change, sometimes out of intellectual curiosity. These motives operate for the collection of data too. Let us take as an example some figures on men, women and employment collected by the British Employment survey (Table 2.1). The balance

TABLE 2.1 Adults, parents and employment: percentage of working-age adults with a job, Great Britain, 1994

	Men	*Women*
Parents*	85	59
Not parents	70	70
All working-age adults	75	65

Note: *People with at least one dependent child under 18.
Source: Derived from 1994 British Labour Force Survey.

of advantages between men and women is one of the most hotly disputed areas in contemporary life and governments everywhere monitor it on a continuous basis.

The type of table of which Table 2.1 is an example is widely used in sociology to make easy comparisons between factors which vary (variables) and to look at their linkage. This one shows that more men are in work when they are parents than when not and the reverse applies to women. It also shows that a greater percentage of men have work than women. How do we explain this? We draw on our knowledge of relations between men and women and advance an explanation, often called a hypothesis, that women withdraw from work when they have children and men take on the responsibility of being the breadwinner. Well this is only a hypothesis which we can research further. So let us gather more information about the relations of men and women and look to the data on parents with partners (Table 2.2). The result shatters expectations. Far from fathers being the breadwinners the data show that mothers are more likely to be employed when their partner is earning and far less likely to be employed if their partner is out of work. In fact even lone mothers are more likely to be employed than mothers with out-of-work partners. We now need to advance further hypotheses to do more research. Our data actually support earlier findings from research by Ray Pahl which showed that with greater equality in the contemporary household the employment of both makes it easier for each. We can't even say which comes first. For instance, joint earnings are high enough to be able

TABLE 2.2 Parents, partners and employment: percentage with a job, Great Britain 1994

Parents	Fathers	Mothers
Partner works	93	68
Partner out of work	74	30
Lone parent	54	39
All parents	85	59

Source: Derived from 1994 British Labour Force Survey.

to afford childcare services. So this may be a couple effect, the outcome of co-operation.

But there are other possible explanations. The fact that so few women with out-of-work partners are themselves in employment hardly suggests new equality when men generally seem so much more easily to stay in employment when *women* are out of employment. State involvement here cannot be discounted. It may simply be that work does not pay for these women if their partner's benefit payment is reduced, especially given that women earn less than men to begin with. It may be that the man's morale is so dented by not having a job that being a househusband too would be the last straw! It may be that some of the women do undeclared cash jobs like cleaning. It may of course also be that they live in areas of high unemployment where jobs are hard to find for both sexes. It may be that women with poor education choose partners with relatively little too – lack of qualifications reduces anyone's chances of finding a job.

We are introducing here, then, the possibility of a lot of new factors – the way the tax benefit system distorts incentives to work, traditional or even sexist values about household roles, the need to know more about the people's characteristics, the general factor of labour market disadvantage for women, perhaps even discrimination against women, or indeed against men getting part-time jobs. We have to do further research – a case of watch this space.

Our example illustrates how the search for explanation is in principle unending, but how equally it is often very important to be able to decide where the weight of evidence tends on the available information. We can't stop the world until we arrive at a 'complete' answer. That time will never come. If the issue is one of economic disincentives then modification of state benefits might be a policy option; if a matter of a culture of sexism, legislation may be considered, or alternatively, and more likely, public information and a continuation of the debates in which men and women resolve the contemporary politics of the family.

Triangulation

Sociology aims to reveal truths about human society. So it builds theories about how societies work and develops methods of studying them which aim to match the intellectual standards of other academic subjects. Every academic discipline develops its own theories and methods to fit the special nature of its subject matter. Human society is not the same as anything else. It is not like the organism, intergalactic space, the economy, the past, nor sub-atomic particles.

So sociology is as different from biology, and from all the others, astronomy, economics, history or physics, as they are from each other. It is also different in important respects from the study of animal societies which ethology pursues.

Sociology has often tried to copy the methods of other sciences, but they all do that. They differ one from the other each in having a different mix, though any one will be shared with another science. The reason the mix differs is because in each case, the topic, the object to which interest is directed, requires it.

The fact of a mixture of methods is not what distinguishes sociology. This is contrary to the view of some sociologists. One has said 'Sociology is a special kind of disciplinary territory. And what makes that territory so unique is exactly the fact that so many different methods ... meet there.'[13] No, the methods are diverse to fit the uniqueness of the field, human society, or social relations.

The borrowing is not just one way either. Some people find this hard to accept for it runs counter to the deep-seated idea that there is a single scientific method, perhaps based in mathematics. But even this can be reversed as the mathematician Reuben Hersh has done by applying an idea of Erving Goffman to explain the intuitive basis of mathematics.[14]

This sharing of methods is true of the ones which capture the popular imagination as belonging to sociology. These are probably the survey where members of the public are chosen at random to answer questions put by an interviewer, or direct observation where a researcher is present in a real life situation and taking notes.

Neither method is peculiar to the subject. The social survey developed through the sponsorship of the state and business and belongs as much to psychology and economics. Observation through involvement, sometimes called participant observation or ethnography, has been the prime method of anthropology.

There is no one sociological research method and there are many other ways sociologists use to collect information which are just as important as these methods but don't come to the attention of the public in the same way. They make considerable use of public documents, both contemporary and historical, but also of more personal records like diaries and letters.

They analyse public statistics which have been collected for special purposes, like accident records, crime or suicide statistics. They are gluttons for text of all kinds: novels, newspapers, advertising materials, minutes of meetings, the contents of files. They may even decide that one good way to get evidence about contemporary views of crime is to watch crime films.

For instance, Robert Reiner, Sonia Livingstone and Jessica Allen studied changes in views of crime in Britain since 1945.[15] They found people once saw crime as an offence against an established and official social order but now are more inclined to set their own standards for judging it. There is a growing emphasis on victims, but also on conflicts within the forces of law and order. The law itself is something on which people are expected to make up their own minds.

These are important findings. They speak of the demystification of authority. This cuts two ways. People have less respect for the law, but they are more prepared to shoulder responsibility. It might suggest to the authorities that crime reduction policies would be best based on enlisting public co-operation rather than to increase policing. This is not the authors' concern, but, once out in the open, their results become a powerful resource in debate. After all, the dominant political rhetoric is to demand greater police numbers.

The researchers used two main methods to collect their evidence. One was to set up focus groups, people brought together and led through questioning into an extended discussion of a particular theme, in this case media treatment of crime. The other was to analyse the content of the media. So the researchers viewed 84 films, examined the place of crime in the top 20 television programmes for each year from 1955, and analysed crime items from two national newspapers on each of ten days in every other year since 1945.

This gathering of evidence of varying kinds and from different quarters has been called 'triangulation', an analogy with mapmaking where it is observation and measurement from different angles which enables the surveyor to fix points and distances. Territorial space has three dimensions, hence 'triangulate'. Social space is more complex with more dimensions which continually merge and separate.

Reiner's research relates crime reports (newspapers) to representations of crime (screen) to opinions on crime (focus groups) in different ways. The interviews in the groups covered reactions to images as well as ideas about the way crime and society had changed over the period. The groups themselves were selected to represent age, class and gender differences. These are variable factors which influence opinions, memories and exposure to the media.

The reason sociological research covers these multiple dimensions is because it is artificial to isolate them. Social reality is not the simple sum of these parts. They are abstracted from it for research purposes and returned to it with greater understanding after the research. We know that they are interwoven. Film makers respond to audiences, journalists evoke scripts, both stories of crime and crime reports shape opinion.

The sharp focus of research casts light on some facets while acknowledging that much remains out of the range of its vision. What about crime reports in the press in relation to actual crimes committed? That would be a different project.

All sociological research balances the need to abstract parts from the whole for the purposes of analysis against the fact that it is the whole which makes sense of the research. The inferences the authors draw about the decline of authority in society are about a condition which pervades social relations generally.

Their work is therefore pertinent to discussions of what happens in school, or in industry, or on the sports field. It becomes relevant to check it against similar research in other countries because there is no reason to think that the underlying processes are confined to Britain. If they are that would itself need explanation. They therefore cross-refer to related research on the media and its portrayal of America.[16] It has connections with the most general theory of the differences between modern and other societies and alludes to the classic theories of crime, law and social integration of Émile Durkheim.

The sheer diversity of data gathering methods which sociologists have adopted on different occasions has prompted hostile comment. This can come from disciplines where a particular method has become the touchstone of scientific worth. So anthropologists can become possessive about ethnography or psychologists about ways of measuring attitudes since they have done so much to develop them.

But unlike those disciplines the direction of sociology has never been led by its research methods, much more by its subject matter. In this respect it is closer to archaeology or history in that neither of those can afford to neglect any possible source of information. But it is not like them in that it is much more led by a conceptual reality, society, and so is closer to law or economics, which begin with analysis rather than a way of gathering data.

Intellectual craftsmanship

The diversity of research methods in sociology is dictated by the nature of the subject it researches, society. Any individual sociologist will have to make appropriate choices within that diversity for any particular project. This is what a great sociologist, C. Wright Mills, called 'intellectual craftsmanship', an essential quality for successful work which cannot be reduced to a set of recipes.[17]

Eileen Barker's study *The Making of a Moonie* is an excellent example of intellectual craftsmanship in sociology.[18] This is not just because of the variety of methods it uses but also in the way the outcome of her research so clearly goes beyond everyday understanding. Her work is much more than intellectual inquisitiveness, which may be intrusive in things social. Often research is the morally responsible thing to do when a topic is shrouded in prejudice.

Barker was drawn into her research partly because the Unification Church was already publicly controversial. Founded by the Revd Sun Myung Moon in North Korea after the Second World War it spread to the United States in the 1960s and was later accused of brainwashing its members, generally known as Moonies, and therefore threatening the traditional family.

For a sociologist this image of the dangerous cult links to a long-term debate within the discipline about the direction of social change and in particular the place of religion in a secular world. When the contemporary world is widely considered to be modern and beyond religion the fact that people become members of religious groups itself brings that view of the world into question. At the same time the public anxiety which this arouses is itself an issue for inquiry. Becoming a Moonie is a fraught social phenomenon.

Barker gained the confidence of a group of Moonies. She tells us how she did this. Her participant observation went through three stages. The first was watching and listening, 'doing the washing up in the kitchen was always a good place for this'.[19] Then she interacted with members by taking part in conversations. Finally she began to argue with them and ask awkward questions.

Often her participation got her into difficulties, like attending a workshop where she was asked to give a presentation on the purpose of the coming of the Messiah. She did so to such good effect that one person present said that she now fully understood that the Revd Moon was the Messiah. Barker explained she did not herself believe this, but it made no difference to the others. She never pretended to be anything other than a sociologist to the people she studied, which meant that reactions to her varied from the accepting to the hostile. But as a sociologist she also represented a link between her subjects and outsiders. Sometimes she found herself drawn into mediating between a Moonie and anxious parents. This in itself says something about the role of the sociologist in contemporary society. There is a need for dispassionate observers with no axe to grind who can be trusted to tell it how it is to them, trained in eye and mind to work according to academic and professional standards.

In this respect the contrast between Barker's approach and that of the journalist is instructive. The stories in the press about the Moonies were almost wholly about the outrage of parents. They might be 'factual', but the facts were those as seen by one of the parties to a conflict. Indeed a newspaper article entitled 'They took away my son and raped his mind' became the subject of a libel action by the British Moonie leader against the *Daily Mail* for false accusation of 'brainwashing'.[20] He lost, and that issue of brainwashing is central to Barker's book. She seeks to establish by close observation how in general people become Moonies. Clearly they didn't accept that they were 'brainwashed', but then their accusers say that is a symptom of their condition. Barker, through close and enduring contact with Moonies without herself subscribing to their beliefs, was seeking to establish a fund of evidence distinct from any that could be brought by the interested parties to a dispute. She was effectively working from the assumption that the sociologist can achieve a certain kind of objectivity.

For her purposes participant observation was not enough. In order to discover whether Moonies were controlled in some illicit way she began by interviewing people who were not in her initial group and eventually distributed a questionnaire to all British members of the Church, gaining 425 replies. She compared those who joined after taking part in introductory workshops with those who didn't, and collected a total of 217 questionnaires. To do this she had to gain access to membership lists. But she also wanted information from people similar to Moonies in many respects who did not join the movement and obtained 110 questionnaires from other sources too. Then, because her work concerned the process of becoming and not becoming a member, contact with those in relations with Moonies was also vital, so she followed up parents and entered into exchanges with the anti-cult movement, with the press and with government officials. But it was not just people who were her source of information. She took their beliefs seriously enough to read and study their publications in depth and treated their accounts not just as personal opinions but as religious statements set in a complex doctrine.

One notable feature of Barker's study is the way it spans a divide in sociological research which often is regarded as unbridgeable, or at least separating two incompatible camps, the qualitative and the quantitative. In the one corner the touchy, feely, understanding type of approach, in the other the hard-nosed, no-nonsense, yes/no, make-up-your mind approach to facts. The first is sometimes called 'interpretative', the second 'positivist'. These also correspond broadly to the two types of sociological research mentioned earlier, the survey and observation.

In point of fact Barker's study illustrates the way these approaches are complementary and overlap such that they are incomplete without each other. She needed to know just how typical members' experiences were to make judgements about the Moonies as a whole, and she needed equally to enter into profounder contact with some to make sense of the more general responses of the many.

In the end Barker concluded that the Moonies were not strikingly different from any other minority religious group. The factors which predisposed people to join were far more important than any unusual technique of persuasion the Moonies might have. The question we are left with at the end is more one of the need to explain the reaction to the Moonies of the wider society than it is to explain the Moonies. Here some wider sociological assumptions about modern society are also brought into question. This again illustrates a thrust of sociology. Its approach to methods is also designed to throw up uncomfortable findings, to disturb taken-for-granted assumptions and to contribute to the continual updating of our understanding of society.

It is the nature of society which dictates the methods we use to find its reality and, because that nature is continually reformulated in and through people's social relations, we can never regard it as fixed and immutable. What counts as facts arises out of those relations. They are social constructions and performances though none the less real for that, and those facts are themselves central to our achievement of understanding of other people. If we say that sociology as a science is concerned with the way people struggle to make society we do not go far wrong. At the same time we can see that sociology can easily become an element in that endeavour.

Professional practice

Ideology and objectivity

By now we can appreciate what a stir it made when British prime minister Margaret Thatcher said that society did not exist. This actually made a lot of people think hard about society, so sociologists should be grateful to her. Thinking often leads to study, and she gave sociology quite a boost, which certainly was contrary to her intention.

Challenging society's existence makes us think, not just about society but also about 'existence'. After all people think about and study a lot of other things which don't 'exist' in the way material things like, say, our bodies exist. For instance, love, values, or God are not material. But not many of us would make sense of our lives without one, two or, many would say, all three of them.

They are not material objects. But then neither are most of the things which interest us about human beings. Consider a speech, meeting or anniversary. They exist in and through what we do. If no one turns up to a meeting which was advertised it doesn't take place. But we don't normally question the possibility of the existence of meetings as a result.

Raising the question of existence brings into the open the fact that different things exist in different ways. Not everything exists on the same plane. Society (meetings included) has its own peculiar mode of being. Mrs Thatcher went on to declare that men and women and their families *did* exist.

Well we can accept men and women perhaps, though we can find problems there too, but what about 'families'? What makes them more real than society? Do they exist as well as the people who belong to them? Then we are into an argument which is about whether individuals are more basic or real than the social units to which they belong. Mrs Thatcher could have quoted many authorities, including Max Weber, the most famous German sociologist, who have said society has no existence outside individuals.

But Weber was active in setting up the German Sociological Association and devoted his career to studying social relations. So his preference for basing sociology on the study of individual social action was really more a statement about the methods of studying social relations than about society's existence.

What he deplored was academics making 'society' equal 'the nation' and then using this as a stick to beat individuals. He wanted to rid the subject of nationalistic ranting, a real problem for the academic world just before the First World War. This illustrates that society is a highly charged political topic. This greatly complicates its study because we can neither avoid nor solve the issues of objectivity and bias which arise. There is no formula which can guarantee that the study of society will be politically neutral. Sociologists simply seek to be as objective as possible by the standards of the academic world, but they can never satisfy themselves fully, let alone the outside world.

For some this poses such a huge problem that they reject the possibility of a discipline devoted to the study of society. But it is not alone among academic subjects in having such difficulties. After all it can't be worse for sociology than it is for the study of politics itself. There are other sciences too which have equally complex, unavoidable problems. The medical doctor regularly confronts issues of life and death which raise moral dilemmas about allowing, not allowing, or helping people to die. We would all be in a sorry state if no one studied medicine because they were unwilling to face the prospect of these inevitable ethical problems in medical practice.

Assertions about human nature or the relations of individual and society provide classic examples of contrasting expressions of different views of the world which each claim universal validity. For instance: 'Man was formed for society' – Sir William Blackstone (1723–80);[21] 'Society everywhere is in conspiracy against the manhood of every one of its members' – Ralph Waldo Emerson (1803–82).[22] Blackstone was an English lawyer, Emerson an American freethinker. This immediately suggests a sociological interpretation. We see them representing contrasting cultures, the stifling conformity of the eighteenth-century English establishment was precisely what the macho energy of the American farmer had rejected. We interpret what is said in terms of the position of the speaker in the wider society. At the same time we adopt an observer's position distant from both. We are relying on a theory which says that a person's view of society as a whole is conditioned by the special place each has in it. This insight is the basis of the long-established sociological theory of ideology.

For sociologists an ideology is a set of beliefs which claims to have universal validity but in fact reflects the social position of its adherents. Views about society as a whole are common components of ideologies. Sociology's view of society as a complex set of social relations, in which people have different positions, allows for changes in those relations and leaves its nature always open to research. The nature of sociology as a science rather than ideology depends not on its achievement of objectivity but on its search for it.

The concept of ideology was the critical response in the nineteenth century to the belief that there were laws governing the working of society which like those of the natural sciences were true for all times and places. To those who objected that society, unlike nature, was founded on individual free will came the reply that moral choice had to observe ethical principles which like natural laws applied universally. Whether society was seen as a set of external forces or as the outcome of human decisions, either way the search was for universal statements.

Not too many universal statements of this kind have been found. 'Who says organization, says oligarchy';[23] or 'the higher the social status the more choice people have' ('beggars can't be choosers') are examples. But these are not very impressive in terms of precision and, while broadly true, exceptions to them abound. Some organisations are democratic and the hobo has choices money can't buy.

Other social sciences appear more impressive in this respect. Economics, for instance, seems to find laws of comparative advantage or marginal utility which can be expressed in precise mathematical terms. But then economists have a different intellectual strategy. The laws they identify hold under certain initial conditions which are never fully realised in the real world. These are abstract models rather than accounts of what actually happens. When commentators (usually not professional economists) declare that the real world always works according to these abstract models events eventually prove them wrong.

But the point about economics today is that the models are tested against data. There is a reality test and economists only ever seek a good approximation between model and reality. It is when they fail to acknowledge the gap between model and reality that ideology critique begins and questions are asked such as: Who employs them? What view of the world promotes their professional interest? In other words their place in society comes into question.

Freedom for values

The idea that knowledge of society must consist in, or be based on, universal truths is very durable. It actually predates modern science and helped to give an impetus to its search for laws. It is tied up closely with religion, with ideas of morality and meaning in life.

The reason is that human social relations are mediated through culture and based in part on shared beliefs about the world and other people. They are not based simply in power or calculation and people's beliefs are factors in the conduct of social relations. We observed this in our discussion of norms in a previous chapter (p. 7). It was illustrated in our discussion of community (p. 44).

Such concepts, when operating to regulate our social relations, are known as values. An everyday idea like friendship exerts an influence on any particular pair of people to the extent that it has a meaning beyond them. Each can appeal to it as something which is widely understood in the society at large.

But reference to other people is not as effective as appeal to a value that is universal. Collectivities in general justify standard practices in terms of values they claim to be universal. The sociologist and philosopher Max Scheler expressed it once as 'My friend may betray me, but friendship lasts for ever.' Indeed it is by the standards of 'friendship' as locally understood that a judgement can be reached on 'betrayal' which people around might accept.

The earliest literary evidence shows that human beings have always been aware of the arbitrariness of these claims. Travel has always shown that customs vary infinitely world-wide. Everyday knowledge of relationships and how they should be conducted is local presuming to be universal. This is how it seemed to Herodotus writing 2,500 years ago:

> Everyone without exception believes his own native customs, and the religion he was brought up in, to be the best; and that being so it is unlikely that anyone but a madman would mock at such things. There is abundant evidence that this is the universal feeling about the customs of one's country.[24]

But how does one resolve differences between peoples of different countries. This is the problem of the diversity of morals. It has challenged the greatest writers and philosophers over the centuries.

Michel de Montaigne, the early modern European commentator on the diversity of morals, suggested that there was a 'law of laws' – namely, behave in the way the place you are in requires. In other words let your behaviour be determined by local practices. That is the extreme relativist position. 'The laws of conscience, which we pretend to be derived from nature, proceed from custom.'[25]

Montaigne's account is in one sense conservative because there are no rational criteria to justify change; in another sense it is liberal in that any locality, however small, can assert its own way of doing things. Like so many of us Montaigne finds the variety of sexual customs fascinating. But in a tourist world the question 'are absolutely all sexual practices permissible?' arises.

The opposite view is represented by Immanuel Kant, for many the greatest philosopher of the modern period. 'Behave always in a way which can be a law for others'– his categorical imperative, or the law for laws – suggests that it is possible for individuals to arrive at universal criteria for right and wrong actions. It subjects all custom to this test and in this sense is critical and even radical. But in its claims to arrive at universal laws it is potentially authoritarian and imperialistic. It opens the possibility for laying down the law for others.

Sociologists cannot avoid this basic human dilemma. But their approach is also a major intervention, for instead of siding with Montaigne or Kant they ask a further question: namely, how in practice do people handle the dilemma in a world where people confront difference of custom and morality on a daily basis?

In this way their work reflects a third philosophical position on morality. Montaigne accepts customs as facts of life, Kant looks to abstract ideals. The pragmatist finds that ideals and facts take on meaning through the human experience of changing social relations. The sociological outlook of the contemporary world has arisen in large part in conjunction with this pragmatism, allied with the conviction that in the flow of human experience there is always the possibility of finding rules for social relations which apply generally. It is this pragmatic universalism which is expressed in the developing law of human rights.

In encounters between people and peoples morality emerges as the permanent tension between fact and ideal and this is a primary human experience. If anything like a universal morality exists it can only be the ongoing achievement of human beings in their relations with each other. If we need a classic statement we can find it in Francis Bacon:

> The parts and signs of goodness are many. If a man be gracious and courteous to strangers it shows he is a citizen of the world, and that his heart is no island cut off from other lands, but a continent that joins to them.[26]

The problem of objectivity greatly exercised the founders of sociology, with the idea that there might be some secure method for achieving it. But that problem was posed initially as if society could be an object like the natural world. Max Weber pointed out that human reality, and that included the social, was cultural and pervaded with values. Facts are the result of people following values and are only important in relation to them. 'Value freedom' in the social sciences on his account could only mean indeed objective accounts of the relevance of facts to values and enhance the chance of choosing between them. In this sense value freedom, far from meaning freedom from values, or neutrality between them, means freedom to choose for them. But this makes society a battlefield of competing values.

After nearly a century of further debate and work sociologists might now reach a rather different formulation. Facts and values and our understanding of them arise out of our experience of human beings in relation to each other. Sociological accounts distil that experience and are most useful when they enable people to come to a greater understanding of those very social relations.

Sociology provides above all a cognitive frame for communicating the experience of social relations. This arises not as a judgement from on high, nor as an arbitration of disputes, nor a wish list. It is the intellectual representation of the changing reality of those relations. In a world which is one it will seek to represent that unity.

Sociological evidence now makes a central contribution to contemporary moral debate. No argument on women's rights, child labour, capital punishment, abortion, worker participation is complete without drawing on evidence of the diversity of experience of these in different places at different times. Protagonists in the debates on such issues, the state, pressure groups, business, charities, will make commissioned research one of the key planks in the case they present.

It is the autonomous reality of society combined with the independence, moral integrity and intellectual capacities of the researchers which guarantees that such research will make a contribution to debates on values and the policies which might implement them. This places a heavy burden on the researcher.

Professionalism

Sociological research places considerable personal demands on sociologists. One set of accounts of doing research provides a catalogue of hazards from conflicts in research teams, stress of interviewing, being caught up in ethnic street-fighting, working under surveillance by prison officers, and being harassed and threatened with libel action.[27] The sociological theory of ideology also ensures that their social position in professional, private or public life can never be discounted and sometimes they do not even feel it ethical to distance themselves. Negotiating this moral minefield is particularly arduous when research focuses on victims and the oppressed. This is an account by Lorraine Radford who researches violence against women:

> The feminist critique of objectivity and distance in social science research had a profound influence upon my approach to research on violence against women. It is not possible, and probably not ethical, to have 'distance' as the top priority when researching a sensitive issue such as the experience and impact of abuse.

Distance seemed to imply that it was possible to switch one-self off emotionally from survivors' accounts of their experiences, maintaining an 'us' and 'them' division between the 'Researcher' and the 'Objects' of study ... I quickly learned however that there are limits to my capacity to 'share the particular pain' of abuse. As a counsellor or therapist, or as someone who can give long term emotional support, I am not up to the job. Distance has been relevant to the ways that I have coped with the personal consequences of doing this type of research and other people's positioning of and responses to my work. Paranoia, fear, anger, aggression, depression, being haunted by memories or accounts of abuse or stalked and harassed by men (and once by a woman) are some of the most obvious personal costs associated with violence research.[28]

Quite apart then from the theory, knowledge and intellectual skills of the discipline which sociologists acquire through university degrees, they need to be both thoroughly versed in the ethics of their work and possess the degree of moral courage which their chosen field of research demands. They have professional associations which draw up codes of ethics for research, provide moral support, a forum for discussion of research and good practice through conferences and journals. They also are useful adjuncts to the job market.

By far the most powerful and influential is the American Sociological Association.[29] In spite of the early importance of Herbert Spencer the British Sociological Association was not founded until 1951.[30] The International Sociological Association was helped into existence after the Second World War by the United Nations.[31] It organises the World Congress of Sociology every four years, the four-teenth having taken place in Montreal in July 1998. The European Sociological Association was set up in 1993 and has a conference every two years.[32]

Compared with many similar professions, these associations do not set the same kinds of tests for membership as say those for psychologists, nor validate qualifications as happens in medicine. Criteria for entry are more like those for a club than for a profession. Interest, contribution and achievement are more important than formal qualifications. There are a number of reasons for this, the main ones being that sociology does not have patients, the care of young and vulnerable people, and does not promise cures. In other words the risk to the public is less, which requires fewer guarantees as a result.

In this respect sociologists who work independently are more like consultants and when they take employment as sociologists they are regularly designated research officers, strategic planners, policy analysts, community development officers, project planners, etc. The result is that it is very difficult to say how many people are employed as sociologists. Indeed the explosion in media-related research, in service occupations of all kinds, in think tanks and the growing sophistication of the relationships between business and consumers, government and publics, coupled with the growth of autonomous non-governmental agencies where sociologists may often take the initiative, means that there is a constant flow of sociologists into work which draws on their expertise.

Thus, while sociologists may compare themselves unfavourably with economists and psychologists in the extent to which they have a recognised professional identity which takes them into a job, they are less likely to be handicapped by being treated as narrow specialists, employable in a restricted range of posts.

But politicians have equally found that sociologists can be useful sounding boards and policy advisers. Raymond Aron was a close confidant of President de Gaulle of France. Mikhail Gorbachev, the Russian leader who led the way in dismantling the Soviet system, was advised by a woman specialist in industrial sociology, Tatiana Zavlaskaya.

The Chinese leader Deng Xiaoping had a friend and adviser who persuaded him and the Communist Party to introduce the new system of agricultural production known as the 'responsibility system' in the 1980s. Fei Xiaotung had studied anthropology and sociology in the London School of Economics in the 1930s, and the new system was based on his studies over decades of peasant life. Since it broke with the previous 'one communal pot' ideology of Chinese communism it arguably has had the greatest effect on the greatest number of people of any policy inspired by a sociologist.

In the United States today the communitarian movement which has influenced politicians of both main parties is inspired by the sociologist, Amitai Etzioni. In Britain the call from Tony Blair to modernise beyond left and right picks up the message from Anthony Giddens, sociologist and Director of the London School of Economics.

Professional sociology can operate in the service of any section of society, for good or bad. However, when working with other professional groups sociologists are bound to be identified with and give expression to those who would not otherwise be heard, be they silent majorities, outcasts or what are now called the socially excluded.

In the late nineteenth century Sumner wrote an essay, 'The Forgotten Man',[33] to draw attention to the hardworking unpraised breadwinner who asked for nothing of the state except to be left alone and in consequence was not heard.

A century later the British sociologist Ann Oakley wrote her book *Subject Women* to make them more than the 'mere shadow discernible in conventional histories and sociologies'.[34] The question she asks, 'Are women people?', could be seen as the rejoinder to Sumner (though he did say 'The Forgotten Man is not seldom a woman'[35]). Oakley and Sumner are each for their time equally driven by the sociological demon.

Lifelong learning

Many different groups of people find varied reasons for looking to sociology. Social workers have always found basic knowledge about how society works relevant, but professionals like doctors and architects also find this has a place in their training. Companies may need to find out more about their employees or about the consumers of their products. Their profits may depend on this.

In the 1980s in Britain when Margaret Thatcher dominated the political scene she and her friends often dismissed sociology as a waste of time. Many threats were made and some were carried through to restrict the possibilities of teaching and studying the subject. Many sociologists feared for their jobs. In fact the subject survived, in some ways even became stronger, as it responded to the threat. The attractions it had for students never diminished.

The blurred boundaries between sociology as an academic discipline, as professional practice and in employment, mean that the question of a curriculum for sociology is always equally open. There is no set of public requirements which insists that every sociologist knows how to do a t-test, conduct a competent interview, or design a research project.

But probably today, as has been the case from the beginning when sociology was first taught in higher education, the main motive for studying the subject has been the individual's sense that society is difficult to understand and even troubling at a personal level. Some people will study it mainly to clear their minds about their own place in society, others more with a mission to do something about it, to repair its failures or promote its successes.

The main contribution sociology has made in the last century is to public consciousness world-wide. You can find sociology anywhere. In 1986 I found a sociology text on the bookshelf of the local policeman, in Bangladesh, in the only brick built house for a hundred miles in a country as poor as any in the world.

Sociology is a much bigger subject than just what sociologists happen to be saying and doing today. It has behind it a century-long tradition of teaching, research and professional activity. So it has informed the thinking of hundreds of millions of people who have studied it in schools, colleges and universities throughout the world.

We can all become sociologists, just as we all can clean our rooms, bake our bread, fish or write poetry. At the end, however, there will be some who want to go further down the road of studying sociology intensively, or even think of it as a possible career choice.

If you do a first degree in sociology in Britain you may avoid technical training, and the common core of your studies is more likely to be regarded as the thought of Karl Marx, Max Weber and Émile Durkheim than any direct experience of social research. This is not widely different in the rest of the world. In the United States there is more emphasis on training in methods of research; in Italy less even than in Britain.

This is not going to change very much. Even if there were a concerted attempt to produce a highly professional sociology curriculum, with common global requirements, it would not affect the basic openness of sociology. It would create an artificial boundary for a certain kind of sociology around which alternatives would soon proliferate. The reader should recognise this as a controversial statement. I am saying that sociology is bigger than what sociologists (including me!) say it is at any one moment. The discipline is produced out of the requirements of contemporary life and its logic develops in response to the nature of society today, not according to some model of what a discipline or professional practice ought to be.

Chapter 3

Sociological
Theory

Old and new directions

The old theoretical agenda

The balance between theory and research in scientific disciplines varies both within and between them over time. There is a division of labour within disciplines between those who concentrate on theory and those who test it out or apply it.

Theory comes first because it needs fewer resources and because it guides the work of the researcher. Historically in sociology it long predates the systematic gathering of data. The origins of the Western theory of society go back to Plato and Aristotle in Athens in the fifth and fourth centuries before Christ. These origins have had far reaching, not to say fateful, consequences.

The Greek philosophers lived in city-states in which the main problem was how to bond a definite group of people into a territorially based community. As a result the long tradition of Western social theory

has largely focused on the relation between the citizen and the agency which controls the territory – the state. This has been the core issue even when generalised as the relation of individual to society.

Lewis Morgan, one of the great founders of anthropology through his studies of Native Americans, even dated the division between ancient and modern society to that time. He reasoned that before the Greeks social organisation was based not on territory and residence, but on kinship – who was related to whom.[1] In our time we tend to associate modernity with the territorial nation-state which developed after the sixteenth century in Europe. But its social and political theory drew its inspiration from the Greeks.

Modern theory now speaks of the nation-state rather than the city-state or the Greek 'polis', but in each case society, people and state are treated as having the same boundaries. It replicates this ordering within the nation-state. The local community, the source of social order and well-being, becomes the local state with local citizens. This tradition of social theory provided the context for the birth of professional sociology at the end of the nineteenth century. Its origins are non-modern, but the nation-state gave it a specifically modern form.

There are two other traditions which have contested the claim which the nation-state made to set the frame for society. One is often thought of as Christian, but it belongs equally to Jewish and Muslim thought – namely the idea of human society, the potential of any human being to relate to the whole of humankind. These religions are universalistic, even though what often strikes the outsider most is their division of the world into believers and pagans, infidels or gentiles.

The other tradition is very specifically secular and modern. It took off in the eighteenth century as political economy and rapidly developed into economics. This line of thought treats society as an ever-extendable network of exchange of goods and services, a market within which a world-wide division of labour develops.

Therefore each of the main sectors of Western civilisation, state, religion and economy had a theory of society embedded in it, with origins in different times and places. The issue for sociology at the beginning of the twentieth century, then, was whether it could define its own distinct approach to society. In the event, even as it struggled to do so, by the middle of the twentieth century, in both Europe and the United States it was the ancient Greek problem of individual and society which prevailed.

The main reason was that the nation-states and the elites which controlled them had already set the agenda on their own terms in the late nineteenth century. For them society was threatened with revolution or at least disorder and decay. The development of the modern industrial economy had undermined long-standing rural communities and the new working class threatened established state structures. It was these issues which the authorities defined as the social problem and it was to their concerns that sociology responded.

With this prompting sociology in Europe, especially in France and Germany, took the decline of community in the face of an advancing modernity as its central problem. The key text for the next hundred years of theory was written by Ferdinand Tönnies (1855–1936) in 1887.[2] Entitled *Community and Association (Gemeinschaft und Gesellschaft)* it contrasted two constellations of social relations, the one where people take their membership as a taken-for-granted feature of their existence, the other where they set up a rational organisation. The latter was the key feature of modernity.

Tönnies' text is probably the most influential and least read classic in sociology. (The closest rival would be Marx's *Capital*.) It provided the elementary ideas for the most famous duo in sociological theory, Émile Durkheim in France, who conceived sociology as an aid to the moral renewal of the country, and Max Weber (1864–1920) in Germany, who was deeply troubled by the threat of capitalism to values of all kinds, especially the nation-state.

There was then a nostalgia built into the foundations of European sociological theory which has never disappeared.[3] By contrast the United States initially looked forward to creating a new future. The early sociologists were enthused by the ideas of competitive struggle from both Herbert Spencer and Charles Darwin. The main agenda item for sociology became the assimilation of waves of newcomers from Europe and the freed slaves into a newly created United States. Later the concerns of the Chicago school of sociology were to find new kinds of communal living in the growing conurbations. Its inspiration was the new European sociology, but in this case

71

the Berlin Jewish sociologist Georg Simmel (1858–1918) whose theory made society a cosmopolitan configuration of social relations beyond the boundaries of national states.

Yet there was also a thrust to declare that the future had arrived. By the 1950s the Harvard sociologist Talcott Parsons had produced a new synthesis of European and American theory which conceived the individual–society issue and social order as the problem of integration into the nation-state. In this frame the local community fulfilled a key subordinate function.

To this day sociological theory in the West is dominated by the individual–society issue, often restated as agency and structure, in the context of the loss of past community. Only recently it has produced a popularised political offshoot known as communitarianism which aims to enhance personal responsibility to the community, and thence to the nation-state.[4]

The contemporary problem for theory

This historical background to Western social theory explains why it is inadequate for the conditions of the contemporary world. Globalisation has meant social as well as economic, political and cultural transformation. Globalisation in a social sense means that the globe provides the space and the boundaries for social relations. The individual/nation-state relation is only one of the major forms of social relation, and community only one of the major possibilities of human association. The new social conditions force us to see how narrow the dominant tradition of Western sociological theory has been if we spell out obvious alternatives.

For a start we should distinguish the individual–society relation in general and for humankind from the issue of relations between individuals and particular societies. Then we should distinguish people's relations with the society to which they are deemed to belong from relations with other societies. Finally we should consider society–society relations.

But 'society' in this classification is only a general heading for a multitude of types of social unit. In each case there is a different kind of relation: individual–community, individual–organisation, individual–movement, individual–class, community–organisation, community–class, and so on. These are not empty boxes. Each has given rise to extensive research. It's just that the theory remains obstinately locked on one variant above all.

These are not paper distinctions. Any manager knows, or should and needs to know, that the workforce, individuals in the organisation, are also individuals in families, that they split into classes, live in communities. Movements too tend to recruit their members from particular backgrounds. It has long been recognised that the Green movement draws its main support from professionals in the public sector.

These multiple reference points then go to the heart of the theoretical problem for sociology which is to provide the propositions which have the maximum scope over time and place for understanding human society in general. Community and association, while broad, are still too narrow in scope. Before Tönnies got to work in Europe, Sumner recognised this in America. 'Political and social events which occur on one side of the globe now affect the interests of population on the other side of the globe. Forces which come into action in one part of human society rest not until they have reached all human society.'[5]

In fact this unity of human society has always been a lesser theme in social theory as far back as the Greeks. Socrates was reputed to have said he was a citizen of the world. Even then it was subordinated to the theme of political community. It was poetic fate that he was condemned to death by the citizens of Athens.

Transformations of the second half of the twentieth century mean that the globe is now a standard reference point. This accounts for the popularity of the idea of globalisation.[6] The encounters of differing cultures with each other are such that the thrust of sociological work has shifted from community to nation and identity. Each is seen as shifting and non-territorial.

Moreover, 'the world' is no longer the West. Cultural encounters are not matters simply of finding ways of tolerating different lifestyles. They involve recognition of differing constellations of social relations. In particular the two major encounters, at least in terms of population size, between China and the West and India and the West, involve two radically different types of society, both from the West and from each other. Each has shown remarkable resilience over two millennia. In each particular social relations are foregrounded.

In China Confucian theory made society an extended family with ruler–subject relations replicating father–son relations, and including marriage, brotherhood and friendship. In India relations between the four historic caste groups depended on mutual obligations which framed both life and death. Before the influence of the modern West neither India nor China conceived of social relations as something to be shaped by the needs of human projects. They were sacred, grounded in the nature of things.

Under conditions of globalisation the agenda for sociological theory in the West is no longer confined to the interests of the nation-state and the local community but extends to the possibility of a frame which will take in India, China, Africa and the rest of the world. But equally globalisation means that those parts of the world may develop their own frames to take in the West! The only concept which is adequate to this task is 'social relations'.

Before Tönnies Marx had put social relations at the centre of his theory of society and insisted both on the primary importance of the social relations of production and in treating capital as a social relation. Among recent theorists Norbert Elias made the figuration of social relations the centre of his theory, although the state was the most important configuring force.[7] Recently Anthony Giddens has focused on interpersonal relations and in so doing raised the issue of the concept of the pure relation.[8] Nearly all the major contemporary directions in sociology can be presented through the concept of the social relation, and this is how we shall look at theory in this chapter.

But, even with the weight of these theories, there is no natural necessity even today for social relations to be foregrounded in public consciousness as a distinct topic. They can be buried from view, under religion, or economy or work. In the West, unlike the civilisations of China and India where they are explicitly safeguarded, social relations are externalities, casualties of economic growth.

When social relations are brought to the surface this is in pursuit of a radical alternative to an existing order of society. This is what happened in the French Revolution with its slogan 'Liberty, equality and fraternity'. Each of these can represent an ideal to strive for. They are equally abstract expressions for the formal relational properties of society. We shall return to this later.

The unit of analysis

When the study of society came to be thought of as a distinct science and not just part of a general theory of humankind, one of the ideas it had to assimilate was the notion of an elementary unit on which to base research. This is an immensely powerful idea, going back to the Greeks who conceived of it as the atom. It is an idea which precedes research. It drives science to trying to find something evermore elementary. So what is now called the atom in physics has long since been disaggregated into even more elementary particles. At the same time the combinations of that unit, the molecule and the cell provide a higher level of complexity and have distinct properties which become the unit of analysis for other sciences, chemistry and biology.

The identification of the unit is important for research methods too. If researchers agree on a unit of sufficient durability which is replicated in differing contexts then they can enumerate them and compare results. They explore their properties through intervention, modifying some and leaving others alone, the basis of experimentation.

As we have just seen from the history of social theory the main candidate for the basic unit in Western sociology has been the 'individual'. There are powerful reasons for this. Western law recognises individuals, though it spoils the apparent simplicity by talking of corporate individuals. The state finds it easy to give each individual a unique number which makes it easy to build databases.

Moreover, if we start with individuals, we build some crucial features into sociology, assumptions like freedom of choice, dignity, responsibility and self-determination. These were some of the reasons which led Max Weber to insist that sociology began with individuals. But there are big problems too.

For a start 'the individual' is an abstract unit. Almost universally societies recognise men, women and children as different in crucial respects. Individuals all have a social nature, which is what

75

makes real people. Second, the individual as choice-maker appears to emphasise rationality and freedom from social ties. Economics developed to make the rationality of choice its special preserve and so this makes society appear as an afterthought or an outcome rather than a precondition.

These references to 'real people', 'freedom' and 'responsibility' make it clear that the question of the beginning *of* a science is not just a question *for* science. The first sentence of St John's gospel, 'In the beginning was the Word . . .', prompted the German genius Goethe to have his anti-hero Faust, driven by an inner demon to search for knowledge, to run through the alternatives: 'In the beginning was the Mind', then 'the Force' and finally 'the Act'.[9]

So Weber himself had second thoughts on this issue and offered, like Faust, an alternative starting point to the individual with the 'action'. So his famous definition of sociology was of 'a science concerning itself with the interpretive understanding of social action, and thereby with a causal explanation of its course and consequences'.[10] The advantage of this formula is that the same act, for example voting or reading, is performed by many people and can be counted. At the same time, as with economic acts like buying and selling, its rationality can be assessed. It enabled Weber to conceive of great constellations of social action and to link them closely to economic activity which was a main concern for him. He was indeed a professor of economics.

There are disadvantages to adopting this rational frame for individual action. It tends to lock people into rational institutions which, Weber conceded, became under modern conditions like an iron cage. Talcott Parsons, who took Weber as one of his inspirations, began with freely choosing individuals – what he called a voluntaristic theory[11] – but then bound them into society by insisting that they had to adhere to its central norms and values.[12] His critics have called Parsons's individuals 'cultural dopes'.

For these reasons Alain Touraine advocates beginning not with the individual but with the 'social actor'.[13] It has the advantages of emphasising both choice and the social qualities of the individual so that social formations, especially social movements, are the outcomes of individual acts. This fits the temper of the late twentieth century much more adequately, but it may still downplay society and the sheer resistance of social configurations to people's wishes. This is often called the facticity of the social and is a feature of all society at all times.

This objectivity of society is what Émile Durkheim emphasised. He went, deliberately, to the opposite extreme and made societies his basic units, treating all social facts as statements about them.[14] So the percentage of people committing suicide is a fact about British society. Durkheim's most famous study was one which compared suicide rates between different societies.[15]

This is effective in reflecting facticity, but not good in allowing for choice, or indeed explaining social difference. After all most people do not commit suicide, and it would be good to have a theory which explained why some do and others don't. In fact it is in relations between people that we find the context, the meaning and the dynamics of the situation which leads to suicide.

In focusing on relations we bring agency and structure together.[16] So my answer to Goethe's Faust problem is 'In the beginning was the social relation'. It is the primary human experience, it defines and sorts objects, and predates ideas. The totality of relations between human beings is the constitution of society.

Power and critique

The problem about social relations is that they don't work just as any one person would like, not even when we are of one will with each other. Sociology has dwelt on many of the paradoxes of these unintended consequences of collective action. The most famous is probably Robert Michels' account of how a political party dedicated to equality and justice like the German Social Democratic Party at the beginning of the century should have generated a powerful oligarchy at the centre.[17]

A cynic might say that it is because people are deceitful and self-seeking. Michels illustrates how with the best will in the world large organisations involve the concentration of power in a few hands. We may want one thing and yet it is another which prevails. In fact we may have a better chance of fruitful change if we disagree with each other, or at the least allow one another to go our own way. Social relations persist and they are embedded in the world so that we tend to reproduce them. Marx's social relations of production in industrial society depended on capital, which in turn reflected the level of development of technology at the time.

So the persistence of social relations depends on material conditions, and the extent to which ideas can penetrate these is limited. Invention can create new conditions, ideals can inspire resistance, but more often than not they seem to reflect the interests of those who gain the advantages from existing social relations, the problem of ideology.

These are famous dilemmas of the human condition, most of which come down to arguments about power. There is a case for saying that this is the most important of all social science concepts, except that it is so pervasive that it appears everywhere. Max Weber complained that it was too amorphous for scientific use,[18] but this can only mean that it is lodged in reality as a major topic not as a technical term.

We need to reflect a little on this amorphousness. If we define power at its simplest as the ability to get something done, we immediately face a distinction between 'power over' and 'power to'. 'Power over' people or things may be negative. It can mean denying people their desires or rights. It can mean burning trees or driving recklessly. 'Power to' looks forward, suggests projects and achievements in which people may be co-opted rather than coerced.

Either way we see immediately that power involves a complex network of links between people, things and projects. As such it is a dimension of humankind's relations with the world and not just a matter of society. What we will find in the discussion which follows of how society is constituted is that power comes in at every juncture, in our use of the mass media, in our personal contacts, in machines, in markets and communities.

With each of these we can talk of 'its power' as well as 'our power' in respect of it. This must be so. They are features of the facticity of the world. Our realisation as human beings involves coming to terms with this at every juncture in our lives. Every science, then, is concerned with power. Even astronomy is concerned to find life in outer space. Sociology's interest in power comes into play at a series of special points. It appears in accounts of technology, ideology or markets, in states and organisations, parties and armies, as coercion or authority, violence or control, domination or hegemony. All are phenomena of power and its exercise.

Power is involved in all social relations, though interestingly it is not necessarily transferable from one kind of relation to another. This is a great area for ironic observations: Citizen Kane, the media mogul, actually motivated by childhood insecurity. 'Dating Agency Founder died a reclusive alcoholic';[19] so business success does not translate into personal success. Or, on the other hand, we have the cynical observation when power does translate from one field to another, as with the Hollywood casting couch. Power may or may not transfer across these types of social relations, but our interest in it, ironic or cynical, is equal, both when it does and when it doesn't.

Famously, Karl Marx treated the power of social classes as the most important kind in human history. In the twentieth century as it has become apparent that classes are not the only or even the dominant agents in human history some have tried to treat human power itself as the subject of history. Michel Foucault was most influential in promoting this view. The problem with this is that it detaches power from any particular agency and removes the points of resistance. It means that only something as generalised as power itself can provide a counterweight. Critique is one main candidate for this position.

Aside from God, from whom science has preferred to keep its distance, critique has been the main hope of intellectuals seeking a source of relief from power. Critique is not the same as criticism or being critical. It is the application of reason to reality, including the use of reason itself. It reveals first principles, but also conflicts of first principles.

It is an idea which goes back to the eighteenth century Enlightenment with its faith in human reason, and then of course back to the Greeks. Marx scorned the idea that reality depended on ideas but he retained 'critique' as a term for any account which showed how reality could be otherwise than it was. In other words critique was to undermine the ideas of a ruling class, their ideological hold on society. Thus it would then open up the possibility of instituting the classless society.

The notion of critique has come to have the meaning of any account which suggests radical alternatives to the *status quo*. These should be possible futures too; critique does not produce utopias. In this form the idea of critical sociology has come to be popular. In fact we shall see that sociology is inherently critical in the sense that it reveals the limits and possibilities which society provides for humankind.

When we point to the way social relations shape our economy, our environment, the way we dress, how we vote and even our sexual behaviour then we point to the essential necessity for it to be possible that things could be otherwise than they are. Sociology does not have to do anything special to be a critique of society. It just has to show it how it is – dependent on effort, resistant to change, threatening to get out of control, always capable of improvement.

The illusion of modernity was that society could be created as the perfect homeland of humanity. It was Plato who dreamed that dream, it inspired Utopia, the French Revolution and the Russian Revolution. In all those cases we find genuine insights into how society works, and then the vain hope that we can make it as we wish. On the basis of those vain hopes interest in society may turn into despair, revolution or, in its tepid form, social criticism. But sociology is not social criticism even if social critics draw on its findings.

In the French Revolution abstract values inspired by pure reason, 'liberty, equality and fraternity', became revolutionary slogans with the idea that society could be shaped to realise them. But they came to incite actions which shamed their advocates. Utopia echoed to the sound of the guillotine's blade. Violence completed the degradation of these values which began when they became slogans.

It has taken a century of sociology to reinstate values like liberty, equality and fraternity – not as goals but as the guiding criteria for sociological research. They are both moral values and cognitive criteria for accounts of society. In other words they belong to science as much as to morality and politics. We turn to that science now.

Constituting society

Ideal types

Sociologists are not professional advocates. They treat values as key parameters of contemporary sociological analysis which establish what we want to measure. This does not mean sociology expects them to be realised, any more than we would expect a cucumber to be straight just because we measure its length. Almost the contrary.

There is nothing extraordinary about this linkage of science and value. What is surprising is that a positivist view of objectivity, that science and values were not associated, should have held sway for so long. It could only do so by insisting that the meaning of 'equality' in nature and society was different. This is nonsense: $1 = 1$ in both cases and for all conditions whatsoever. What does differ is our interest in equality, whether we strive for it in some special area, or whether we measure how far conditions of some kind approximate to it. We can for instance measure income differentials, or we can strive to reduce them. We are concerned in each case with the same condition of inequality. It's a measured fact and a value condition at one and the same time.

The result is that it is impossible to do sociology without engaging with social inequality, for all sciences undertake measurement of equalities and inequalities in their own sphere of interest. Interest in society unavoidably involves measuring social inequality. Sociology is therefore inherently critical as its opponents rightly perceive. If you want to leave society undisturbed by critical accounts then sociology has to be suspended.

It is inherent in our research that we show the conditions and causes of inequality, the varieties of unfreedom and how communities are formed. We might then have the chance to be more effective in our interventions. In this section we review the core ideas in contemporary sociological theory under three main headings: mediation, sociation, and structuration. These roughly parallel liberty, equality and fraternity. Indeed the affinities between the old terms and the jargon might well prompt us to question the need for the new.

However, though the old terminology has its place in political rhetoric sociology's concern has been to find the conditions for their realisation and it is these realities to which our technical terms refer. Sociological theory is concerned both with the logic of social relations and also with their reality. This is important because the logic leads us into unending chains of reasoning and we need to know when to stop for practical purposes. For research and other practical purposes we stop when we feel we have gained sufficient understanding of a concrete configuration.

So if we take power we try to elaborate its sense in the abstract, which means for any time and place. It is then purified of contamination by local or ephemeral features. But if we want to understand the power of Rupert Murdoch or George Soros, then we need to know how power is lodged today in the ownership of global capital, control of mass media corporations, and how it operates through global financial institutions.

Relations between people operate through the shared experience of an outside world. All social relations work through this medium. The only relations which do not are mathematical or logical. In this sense there is no such thing as a 'pure' social relation. This doesn't mean to say that we don't look for purity, but it is always something which is negotiated in real social relationships. And the reality comes through feelings, ideas and objects. Strip away these features of the real world and you are left with abstractions.

If, for instance, we consider equality and inequality in a pure sense this is a mathematical notion. As *social* relations they always have to be expressed in terms of differences in opportunities, talent, wealth, or esteem. If we consider liberty, which can also be expressed mathematically as a constant, a factor which is unaltered by changes in other factors, then in human affairs this has to be seen in terms of independence in respect of others, and then it becomes always a matter of degree.

Fraternity is more difficult to express mathematically because it is paradoxical, but we do so in the statement 'the whole is greater than the sum of the parts'. We are dealing with effects which only operate when units of an aggregate operate together. Eight people combining to lift an object will achieve much more than each one of them taking it in turns. The combination of capitals works in the same way as the most important collective force of modernity.

Mathematics and logic are tremendously powerful tools for scientific work, but they are aids to understanding society, not to be confused with its reality. Weber pointed out that if we have pure, clear concepts we can advance our understanding. He called them 'ideal types' because they were pure ideas (like the 'straight line') never to be found in their purity in the real world.[20]

From the scientific viewpoint ideal types are not ideals to be pursued, though they might well be for some people. For Weber the most important ideal type was the purely rational economic agent, and economics has become the most successful social science in applying models of pure rationality. But no person or firm, however much they might seek to be so, is purely rational. No room is ever truly square as anyone who has tried to fit a carpet has found.

Weber was right to emphasise the essential uses of pure concepts but he neglected the fact that it is not only scientists and intellectuals who work with pure notions. People do so in everyday life. This criticism was made by the sociologist, philosopher and banker Alfred Schutz in one of the most important books in sociology.[21] He emphasised that we all interact on the basis of stereotypes, or typifications, images of our society, idealised versions of ourselves and others, hate objects as well as heroic figures.

Weber would have replied that these everyday concepts are less than purely rational. But Weber was over-impressed by the pure logic of economics and the clarity of legal formulations. Economists and lawyers are not necessarily the most successful business people. As a practising banker, Schutz was aware that ordinary people also work on the basis of their own ideals and pure concepts and try to make them work out in practice. His work only became widely known in sociology in the 1960s, and with its stress on everyday rationality provided a major justification for finding out how people actually behave, which had an affinity with the democratic demands of that time. As so often happens political movements and intellectual insights found points of common concern.

As soon as we talk about 'everyday rationality' it becomes clear that we are dealing with a vast variety of ways in which people conceptualise familiar ideas. We can talk of 'the family' in the abstract but even within a particular society no one family is identical to another.

If we are going to talk sensibly about families and to theorise about them then we have to recognise this diversity.

We will acknowledge different types of marriage, types of relationship which are similar in many respects, like partnership or cohabitation, and the fact that some people are not in any of these. We will recognise the cultural relativity of the family and not expect there to be one right way. We will keep clear in our minds the difference between the ideal we might have of the family and a pure concept as employed by sociologists.

Mediation

The reality of social relations is a human achievement maintained through our senses and the ways in which we express ourselves in and through the material world. We can perceive this embeddedness of relations in reality through the notion of 'media', which is the plural of 'medium'. But it is these material and social limits on human expression which mean that an idea of pure freedom hovers over any discussion of media.

A medium permits in some way information about two or more subjects to be conveyed between them. In a seance the spiritual medium acts as the go-between for us and a spirit world. A mediator is the medium for reaching agreement between the parties to disputes. Oil paint was the medium Rembrandt used for conveying to posterity his gaze on his own day. Print is the medium for the mass circulation of writing, hence mass media like newspapers, radio, television. A currency is the medium for exchange.

From these varied but cognate senses of medium we recognise that communication is common to them all. Just as power is a feature of the relations between humankind and the world in general, so communication is a feature of all social relations. It exists in tension with power, and it represents a different kind of relation. Power as a relation involves causation, mechanical effects. A relation involving communication permits a degree of free and reciprocal expression. In short we feel that communication is more human than power.

Communication is involved in all our bonds. For a message to be delivered, both have to speak the language and get to the telephone.

For lovemaking each has to learn where the other person likes to be touched and be able to recognise the right moment to touch. To agree a loan, the lender checks your account and the borrower needs to know the going interest rate.

So vital is communication to human society that again, as with power, some have tried to make this the essence of society. But communication and power do not necessarily flow in the same direction. Power may depend on communication, but often enough distorts it. Sometimes power is exercised precisely by excluding people from information, and the control of media is power. Foucault stressed always that it is power which establishes the very terms of discourse.[22]

Because power distorts communication Jürgen Habermas, the most influential German social theorist of the late twentieth century, has argued that the just society will only arise when there is an equalisation of power so that there can be full and free communication.[23] But if this is interpreted to mean that everyone communicates with everyone all the time, in the resulting babel no one would hear anybody else. The inference might then be that we need unequal power in order to communicate.

I think that is a dangerous conclusion to draw. It may well be that the freedom implicit in full communication is in permanent tension with its own essential requirements. It depends always on a medium which is accessible to the parties and belongs to their reality. But if we see social relations defined exclusively by power and communication then the only choice of society we appear to have is between a communication utopia or fascism. There are other things in social relations. In co-operation, for instance, power and communication are involved, and also a common will which is not reducible to either. But participation in common projects is selective, dependent on knowing who is in and who is out, even if membership is freely available.

A huge apparatus of law and institutions builds up around the tension between power and communication. It is the basis of the legal principle of informed consent. When President Clinton denied that he 'caused contact with Ms Lewinsky's genitalia or breasts' he explained that he understood that 'cause' implied 'forcible behaviour'. The problem then becomes that it raises the question of what kind of relations did exist since he also denied having 'sexual relations'. A British journalist calls these statements 'baffling wordplay'.[24] They certainly are the outcome of a kind of play – the interplay of law and society.

Sociological theory accepts the principle that human beings find their own solution to these dilemmas in their own way. The author communicates with the reader through the book. Frustratingly you can't be sure about my intentions and I can't be sure I have made myself clear to you. This always appears as a constraint on freedom even as it permits communication. The book itself sets the limits of our understanding each other. Of course if we could begin a dialogue over the Internet then the possibilities of understanding change. But we never escape a medium of some kind. So important is the channel of communication that in the words of Marshall McLuhan (1911–81) 'the medium is the message'.[25]

You might think that perfect understanding might be possible if we could only talk together. But it is an illusion to think that there is communication without a medium. Language itself is a medium, the sound, the grammar, the vocabulary without which we cannot reach understandings, but yet frustrates us in not having the right word for our thoughts and feelings.

When we go beyond spoken language with signs and gestures we still use physical media and rely on the senses which are common, the deep meaning of common sense. In what for many is the most intense communication with another, lovemaking, the surface of the skin is the main medium. Yet we can never be sure . . .

There is a long history of thinking about society which says that the deepest, most authentic and rewarding relationships are ones which rely on communication with someone in their presence, at its most rewarding when there is physical contact. These are what, following Pitirim Sorokin,[26] we can call sensate relations.

We can contrast these with ideational relations. So a parent–child relation and that between lovers are sensate relations, while student–teacher and senator–citizen are ideational relations. There are other ways to express such a contrast. Some have described the one as primary, the other as secondary, which suggests a time order; infancy as opposed to adulthood, or preliterate societies compared with our own today.

So this is a distinction which brings along both a theory of individual development and also historical narrative. At one time this might have been called the story of human progress, but sociologists in general have taken the pessimistic side of modernity's outlook on the future. They have been inclined to think that when relations are ideational the more society becomes removed from fulfilling important emotional needs. This is particularly the case when they consider the ideas embodied in technology. The worker in the textile factory is engaged in bodily labour but with physical objects; relations with fellow workers depend on the product of that labour, not on their ideas about each other and still less on their feelings.

Of course ideas are there: the looms are the product of ideas, but not the ideas of the workers working on them. They stand next to each other, overseen by a foreman, under the manager's surveillance, employed by a capitalist. These are the 'social relations of production' made famous by Karl Marx. They are hardly social at all for the workers themselves who, in Marx's terms, are alienated from them. But they are still in definite relations with each other, positioned in a production system. The machinery becomes a medium for their relations.

This idea of alienation became central to the critique of modern industrial society because it drew attention to the disappearance of old types of social relations where people produced for their own family's consumption or served others directly, or made objects which they sold. The factory system replaced these with work for wages on products the workers did not own, for people they would never see.

It was a critique of industrial society shared by radicals and conservatives alike which depended on nostalgia. Radicals looked back to a primitive communism such as Lewis Morgan described, conservatives to a feudal past, a society in which everyone knew their place. In each case they felt it was possible to recover what was lost.

Nostalgic critique devalues the present and, since the present is the only time we have on earth, this is depressing or inflammatory. However, it carries an important message, which is that if society as such is too low on our priorities and is pushed out by another life-sphere, such as the economy, technology, religion or the state, then we will lose out on profound satisfactions in human existence.

It is possible to have optimistic critique however. Robert Pirsig's book *Zen and the Art of Motorcycle Maintenance* tells how a father establishes relations with his son by way of mechanics. It suggests that shared mastery of the daily conditions of our lives is not out of reach. In this case Pirsig looks for inspiration not to some primitive state, nor to medieval times, but to ancient Greece and a range of virtues which can kick in whenever we take charge of our lives and explore the media of our relations. But it is a search: 'We're related to each other in ways we never fully understand, maybe hardly understand at all', declares the narrator at the end.[27]

Yet the advance of technology is so rapid we are continually facing the loss of control. We are forced into a permanent state of ambivalence towards change. New kinds of information technology advance systems of impersonal control and surveillance in connection with finance and the state. Our experience of cash cards, ticketing, entry codes, ID numbers, credit ratings is one of an external system penetrating our lives. Habermas describes the way systems penetrate not just our work situation but also the fabric of everyday life as 'colonization of the life-world'. It is the extension of what some have called 'system integration' rather than 'social integration', when societies are organised around felt relations or shared ideas.[28]

Technological development does not only facilitate control and co-ordination of systems of relations, it also facilitates the mobilisation of people as individuals. The importance of the mass media is that they provide symbols and enactments of a generalised image of the wider society for local and private consumption. They thus provide the means to realise the opposing tendencies in a mass society of apathetic individualisation or mass mobilisation for causes.

None of these technical advances in communication is as impersonal as social relations mediated by money in a market when any two people can calculate the benefit they get from a deal compared with what they might get in an alternative deal from a hypothetical third person. Both new technology and currency are sometimes taken as examples of the growing dependence of social relations on abstract systems. This recalls an older critique of modern society generally as abstract and removed from human need and sensate relations, associated especially with the philosopher of science Karl Popper.[29]

We have to recall the tendency to pessimistic nostalgia in critiques of old modernity at this point. There is an upside too. In the wake of creating the mass media the new technological means of communication produce countervailing possibilities to old modern forms of central control. The colonisation of the life-world actually enhances personal skills in computer use and information gathering. The Internet and e-mail have opened up new possibilities for information dissemination by radical movements and for maintaining personal relations over indefinite distances.

We have distinguished four broad types of media of social relations: sensate, ideational, technological and abstract systems. It is tempting to see them as successive stages in a history determined by technology. But we should recall our reflections on human collectivities in Chapter 1 at this point: factories, universities, hospitals, offices. Technology always involves configurations of social relations and in collectivities all four kinds of media are combined in different ways. In other words our four types are 'ideal types' in Weber's sense and are always mixed and fused with material things in the real world. Thus all social relations are sensate to some degree. A telephone conversation about the stock market between New York and London involves just as much aural contact as one between next-door neighbours.

Liberty means recognising conditions, opportunities and limits on choice, including other human beings and the choices they make. We have hinted at this already, but only indirectly. In fact our four types of mediation recognise these limits rather unevenly. Sensate relations are often thought of as consensual, both parties consenting, until one remembers violence is also sensate. Ideational relations again also are often thought of as behaviour in terms of shared values or views of the world until one remembers state propaganda.

Technical relations appear to exclude choice altogether as a factor to consider, and with abstract systems we think of surveillance. But we can think of the freedom of e-mail and the choice in 'free' market relations. The quote marks around 'free', however, alert us to the ideological significance of treating the market or indeed any form of mediation as a matter of liberty alone. We then forget what media do. They provide the means for communication in social relations where people interact. Free choice then is conditioned not just by media but by other people, and this is where we confront the problem of inequality.

Sociation

We now come to the pure modes of social relation, remembering that they never can appear in pure form but are always mediated. Two of the most discussed are co-operation and conflict, partly because they are dilemmas in everyday life but also because they are universal in human society, and arguably in animal society too. Coercion and exchange are closely linked with them, which brings in questions of power and authority. We will stay with this limited set of pure modes in this section. They sharpen our focus on the question of equality.

The word 'sociation' conveys the processual nature of these relations. They never stay still. They apply to couples or to sets of relations, or indeed to whole organisations. Social relations are multiplex, that is they operate for different contexts simultaneously.

If we take an exchange between two people we can consider it in terms of their interaction at the time, whether it is in good faith, in terms of their relationship (that is, the past history of their interactions), in terms of the positions they occupy, as buyers or sellers, or as agents for an organisation, as well as in terms of the widest scope of society as man and woman or citizens of the world.

All relations involve questions of balance, of 'more or less' as between the parties to the relation, so that in every case the question of equality arises. But we know very well that the kind of equality we talk about in love is different from what we discuss in coercion. Employers and trade unions may be locked in a conflict with a balance of power. They may be exercising equal coercion on each other, but it is not a love match.

There are also questions of distance which are not about equality. We understand very well the difference between close and distant kin relations, which has nothing to do with geographical proximity and everything to do with the extent to which we take particular other people into account in what we do.

In society we move in social space, where there are many kinds of location. We can distinguish for instance our position relative to other particular persons from our place in a set of social positions which are more enduring than the individuals who occupy them. You have your friends at work, but your job means you do regular business with many others in the firm. There are also relations with society in general, often the least understood. We mentioned these with the mass media, but any person identified as a worker, or a citizen, or a woman, is set in relation to society as a whole which can extend world-wide.

Friendship groups, often disparaged as cliques in politics, are sets of interpersonal relations; positions in government are engaged in enduring functional relations. But these are all social relations, mediated in different ways. What makes political intrigue intriguing is the way politicians weave cliques and office together. Sociologists delight in exploring these interconnections, which are often designated in legal terms as conflicts of interest, but which sociologically are normal features of complex society. The clashes between them often appear as 'corruption' when individuals are unable to manage the separation of private relations from public duties.

In sociological terms what lawyers do is to invoke rules for social relations of a third kind in order to regulate the conflicts between the first two. We can see then three orders of social relations at work, the first being interpersonal, the second organisational, the third societal. They operate in all of us at the same time, with hugely varying scope across different and overlapping groups. Societies are vastly complex constellations of social relations.

The social relation on which historically most faith has been pinned as a counter to inequality is co-operation. Free and equal contribution to a common life according to differences of ability has from Aristotle to Karl Marx been regarded as the strongest form of society. By co-operation we mean joint effort to sustain a social relationship or a group. In the fullest sense it means that the relationship or group operates as a single unit and its products or effects can be regarded as common to the individuals who participate. It's the team which wins and not just the goal scorers. Both community and organisation depend on co-operation to mitigate their inherent inequalities.

At the same time co-operation between some may involve conflict with others. The pursuit of common purpose, even where it is not explicitly designed to subordinate another group, may involve conflict over scarce resources. Simmel pointed out that conflict between groups sustains solidarity within them. To this extent the institutionalisation of conflict in forms of market competition or collective bargaining in contemporary society may result in greater effort, something which exponents of the virtues of markets have stressed.

Co-operation in the market as involved in acts of exchange is balanced by the competitive relations between rivals for the same partners in exchange. Out of this balance develops the division of labour and the proliferation of specialised occupations which for Adam Ferguson and Adam Smith in the eighteenth century were the basis of civilised society. 'It is not from the benevolence of the butcher, the brewer or the baker that we expect our dinner, but from their regard to their own interest' was Smith's famous dictum.[30] For Smith self-interest meant co-operation in the market. The wider the market the more extensive the bonds between human beings until they covered the world. This is a long way from the popular prejudice that Smith somehow favoured rampant individualism.

But it was an optimistic view of market society which depended on the prior establishment of conditions for peaceful trade. This depended on political community, where the sovereign had the prime duty to defend the nation and uphold its laws. Confidence in public order was therefore a general precondition for economy and society.

On the face of it two diametrically opposed principles come into opposition when we consider the market and the state, the one depending on peaceful exchange, the other on force, one on equality and consent, the other on inequality and coercion. It is these fundamental social relations which underpin both these institutional areas before either can be pursued as a technical interest in economics or law.

The most important sociological contribution to solving this contradiction is still probably Max Weber's theory of legitimacy. Rejecting coerced equality, the system of state socialism, even before it had been instituted anywhere, as unworkable, he advanced a view that consent to inequality was the source of social order in all complex societies. We accept orders from others because we believe they have the right to issue them.

In modern societies the most important example of legitimate order is bureaucracy, which is common to both capitalist organisation and the state. Here officials implement instructions which have a legal or technical basis which people accept in a routine way. The common interest in bureaucracy of both state and capitalism meant for Weber that this was the dominant form of large-scale organisation in modern times from which there was no obvious escape.

Apart from bureaucracy Weber saw legitimate authority, the belief that it is right to obey, as a universal feature underpinning all kinds of social relationships, from the workplace, to the family, to the sect. Authority we may say is a universal. The consequences of an unqualified acceptance of this position are frightening. They can mean uncritical acceptance of evil. We can illustrate this from the famous work of the social psychologist Stanley Milgram on people's inclination to obey others.[31]

Milgram found that an inclination to obey was prevalent even where it did not appear to serve individual interest and even where it ran counter to moral views. His research involved a mock-up of a laboratory, where subjects had to follow a scientist's instructions to administer corrective electric shocks to a learner. The majority were prepared to do so even at risk of severe physical harm to the learner because they felt that someone else had the responsibility.

His research has profound implications for, and arises out of the debate about, the causes of the Holocaust. It suggests that this crime against humankind could arise simply out of a routine obedience to orders rather than prejudice against the Jews. If this is the case it could be an enduring tendency which may come out in diverse circumstances and not just in the extreme conditions of the Second World War.

So might not this obedience be a characteristic of individuals which is so prevalent that it determines the kind of society we live in? Certainly Milgram was interested in it as a quality of individuals and in demonstrating its prevalence. But he too acknowledged that his work depended on setting up and exploring one particular type of modern social relationship – that between scientist and non-scientist.

So the experiment may equally demonstrate the layperson's general belief in the professional and moral superiority of the scientist. Milgram's research originated in his interest in the Holocaust. Its results back up Zygmunt Bauman's argument that it is the general presumption in favour of science, rationality and its agents which in modernity turns even Nazism into a routine everyday implementation of rules and regulations.[32] Naive trust in science may make any end acceptable, however evil.

We can see how the organisation of science allied to Weberian-style authority, unquestioning obedience, has the potential for the Holocaust. But there are countervailing factors. Authority itself need not come in such unequivocal form. In the contemporary organisation it has to depend more on mutual respect and professional understanding than on unquestioning obedience.

Nor does the great organisation, community or society have to be so unequivocally organised from the centre. Far from an inevitable trend to the great hierarchies of bureaucracy the contemporary world exhibits a far greater emphasis on lateral social relations, networks of competent people. Often mistakenly viewed as pure markets, these are also associations of like-minded people with many purposes in common. Moreover, since the operations of markets always generate inequality out of equality even as they enhance efficiency, the associations of contemporary society are the best guarantee for the preservation of that degree of equality which is necessary for common humanity to prevail. Yet utopia is not around the corner. The best-run organisation and the most harmonious association are always cross-cut by cleavages.

Structuration

The word 'structure' has often been used for the factors which divide people in society as opposed to relations which link them. Occupations, class, gender, age, place, can all structure the likelihood of people entering relations with each other. For any society these appear as regularities over time. Moreover, while they divide people, none the less the processes of division require the active engagement of people in their reproduction. 'Structuration' as a term has been promoted by Anthony Giddens to convey the sense of continuous construction, of change as well as of stability.[33]

For instance, accounts of relations between light- and dark-skinned people in any country point to the relative disadvantages and exploitation of the latter by the former, which affirmative action seems unable to remove. But the degree of relative deprivation does change as a result of forces which governments may not control. So apartheid in South Africa has gone as a result of a combination of forces: resistance, capitalistic interests and a world-wide movement of support for the cause of the black people.

Older ways of considering structure considered divisions in society or described institutional bias, but each kind of analysis on its own tends to be static. Dividing people by social characteristics seems to close down on their active engagement in society. Accounts of institutions seem to emphasise the way they reproduce themselves. Neither approach on its own brings us to the point of accounting for the collapse of apartheid society. This in itself is a justification for using the term 'structuration' rather than 'structure'.

For the question which concerns us in understanding how society changes is not how many people fall into which category, or how they engage in standardised activities, but rather how the categories and activities themselves are constructed and reconstructed. We may know how many people are dark- or light-skinned; we may also know how people get jobs: but structuration involves the construction of ethnicity and racism as real obstacles to gaining a job.

There is a feature of older analyses of structure which structuration theory takes forward. When sociologists showed that people were divided by age, gender, ethnic origin or occupational status they drew attention to factors over which people have no control. They may have distinguished between ascribed and achieved status; you can't help getting older, (unless you 'end it all' prematurely) but you may gain a better job. But the job normally exists first before you get it. So although these features are treated as original or acquired properties of individuals, they are the divisions of society.

They are also cleavages which cross national boundaries and cut through social relations. Going back to our distinctions between first-, second- and third-order social relations (p. 91), broadly those of the third order cut across first-order ones. Indeed our main types of social relation – co-operation, coercion, exchange – can be constructed afresh in every interpersonal situation. But we are not in a position to change our age, gender or ethnicity in the same way.

This has to be one of the most frustrating things in interpersonal relations. Time and again we find that we are shut out from a fully satisfying relation with someone because we are of different classes, nationalities, age, sex or gender. Conversely we may be thrown together with someone on the basis of sharing these characteristics and find we can't stand each other.

These are the cleavages of the wider society which we work out in personal relations. When speaking of 'the politics of the family' sociologists don't refer to what politicians say about the family, which, with due respect, has little impact on our daily lives, but the way in which, in our households, as individual people we struggle to achieve a balance between society's definitions of the relations of men, women and children and what our own wants and particular situation require.

These struggles are set in the flux of societal relations, which no longer appear under anyone's control. At one time social problems were seen as solvable through government measures, because it was assumed the nation-state fixed the parameters of society. Once societal cleavages are recognised as features of society which are outside and beyond country boundaries these problems are recast. Poverty, unemployment, poor housing, drugs become matters of social relations. This is why these issues are now grouped together under the heading of social exclusion.

I have argued in my book, *The Global Age*, that globalisation is the impetus for refocusing attention on society as distinct from the nation-state. Indeed with hindsight we can see it was the hidden prompt for recasting the theory of social structure as structuration, even though Giddens developed structuration theory before he turned to globalisation.

But globalisation only draws to our attention what is always the potential of human society; namely, for the widest cleavages to be worked out in personal relations or, put another way, for the global to be local. It is the reworking of social problems as issues of exclusion and inclusion which suggests that in structuration theory we are really exploring the possibility of realising the old ideal of fraternity. For, effectively, in discussing the sources of cleavage we are concerned with the formation of bonds, or who belongs and who does not, and how inclusion and exclusion arise.

At one time this was thought to be a question of community or national society. Class was seen as divisive and disruptive and the end of class division became the implicit goal of social theory. It was class, and in particular the rise of the working class, which was seen as the big social problem and the solidarity of the nation-state was seen as the solution. In the work of Émile Durkheim fraternity became solidarity and national integration.

The importance of structuration theory is that it makes it obvious that these issues span community boundaries and that exclusion and inclusion are processes which go on all the time. They are not fixed once and for all, nor are they unilateral and unequivocal. The main features of structuration cross both community, regional and national boundaries and each other. Ethnicity, gender and class divisions do not coincide and they are not confined within nation-states.

Cleavage does not necessarily mean conflict. People can simply avoid others – say ignore the beggar in the street, never cross the other side of the railway tracks – or they can convert cleavage into ritual distance as in the Hindu caste system. But it does mean that the potential for free and equal communication across the divide is minimised, and hostility and open conflict are barely suppressed. It is these conflicts that the nation-state seeks to control, sometimes through welfare, sometimes by encouraging nationalism.

Nationalism depends on the vain aspiration to create the same kind of fraternity which can only be realised in interpersonal relations. The best that can be achieved with nations is playful personal identification, as in national sport, one of the great innovations of the twentieth century. The national bond is a third order one between people who do not know each other. Where zealots and bigots try to make third-order relations govern first-order ones savage results are often the outcome. The members of so-called mixed marriages, across ethnic, class, or religious divides can become tragic victims of societal cleavage which degenerates into violence, as we have seen in Bosnia and Northern Ireland.

In global society men and women do not marry simply on the basis of complementary sex and gender definitions, even as defined by their own culture. They seek to find their own definition of the relationship which makes it unique to them. This has its problems: for Western societies, where the constant interpersonal negotiation may never come to a conclusion or results in breakdown and divorces; or for older cultures where family conflicts arise when children resist parents' attempts to impose their definitions on their marriage. Age and gender are potential sources of cleavage for any society. So too is ethnicity when it doesn't coincide with national boundaries, and normally it does not. The other most important bases for cleavage are class, interests, values and status.

Class cleavage arises out of capital accumulation and market opportunities. On class sociologists exhausted themselves and everyone else in the 1960s and 1970s, mainly because, whether they were on the left or right, they were concerned with Marxist predictions of the polarisation of society around two classes: capitalists and workers. Class remains important, but not polarised, and it is overlaid by other cleavages.

Interest groups are phenomena of the pursuit of political power and operate where the state can be influenced. Just as with class, public attention tends to be directed away from broader phenomena and on to prominent but rather minor examples. So we read a lot about organisations which lobby in Congress or Parliament. But the broadest interest groups are defined by their relations to tax and employment. Public sector employees, state pensioners, top-rate taxpayers are examples of such groups. But the most important interest group of all is the political elite itself, those who live from office in government.

Value cleavage has its obvious forms in religious groups, churches, sects and denominations. The contest between church and state to define society is one of the longest-standing cleavages in the Western world. At the present time, however, there are many commitments – to peace, women, rain forests, environment, human rights, animal rights – which cut across boundaries and relations and are not aligned with traditional religious affiliations. In so far as these movements have replaced those that are based in class, some sociologists have described them as post-materialist.

Finally status, the ordering of people and positions in society according to esteem and respect, cross-cuts all the other cleavages. Indeed it is to some extent paradoxical to call it a source of cleavage because in giving relative rank to politicians, entrepreneurs and priests it is the most purely social of all kinds of structuration. But it is a selective criterion in forming social relations, different from power, and it also reduces breadth and scope of communication. Like the other forms of structuration it crosses boundaries. While there is cultural variation in status ordering, professional people for instance will normally enjoy high status wherever they travel in contemporary society.

Boundaries and identities

Difference

There was a decision in September 1998 in an Egyptian court of justice to overturn a government rule that wives could not leave the country without their husband's consent.[34] In the particular case a woman was seeking to become a teacher in another Arab country. This judgement reflects not so much modern influences on Eastern cultures, but global effects on modern cultures. For the original government ruling in Egypt was only 24 years old and reflected the thrust of a modern state to seek both to regulate marriage and control its borders.

Human society has always been divided into societies which have sought to provide an envelope for people from birth to death. These societies seek to represent society in general and try to contain within themselves the sources of cleavage we have just described. In so doing they produce the biggest cleavage of all. They become 'peoples' or 'countries' as we described them in Chapter 1. In their mutual recognition in the modern world we have what is called the international system.

But when we take the globe as a whole we recognise that human beings are never just members of a particular country or even of a limited number of societies. By virtue of belonging to the human species they are social beings and belong to human society as a whole.

99

At the same time they are equally individual members of the species and belong to humankind. As individuals they are more than just social, and as the sum of individuals humankind is more than society.

These simple statements are controversial. The social is often set against the individual. But you can't be individual without being social. Yet being individual marks you off as having unique qualities which distinguish you from other human beings. Contemporary sociologists have recast this age-old discussion of the balance between individual and society in terms of the ideas of identity and difference. This is the new sociological understanding of the relations of individual and society, where they are not opposed to each other but treated as essentially linked aspects of human social life.

Difference develops through the moves people make in, across, and between social units of all kinds, societies, associations, groups. They acquire the markers of the distinctiveness of those units. So the unique biography of a person is a personal history of relations with other people and of the acquisition of characteristics, each one of which others may also have but which together make a unique set and a very personal experience.

The nearest analogy to this process of individualisation in society is with speech and language. A language is a common resource where we acquire personal competence only by talking with others. The distinction between the language as I have acquired it, my vocabulary and expressions, and the shared language of myself with others is one arising not from opposition but from dialogue. Equally, just as languages may be distinct in different societies, language in general belongs to humankind as a whole and any particular language is potentially open for learning for any individual from any part of the globe. Culture is a common resource for humankind.

Sociologists do not deny individuality, nor the biological uniqueness of each individual. However, they do stress that it is only in and through the experience of social relations that individuality of any kind, physical or mental, can develop. The dependence of human beings on social relations is so profound that when we separate them in words we generate all kinds of paradoxes. Talking of individual and society as distinct things pushes us to thinking of bodies and biological uniqueness on the one hand and collective action and state control on the other, just to keep them separate in our minds. But they are inextricably interwoven.

Collective action is only evident in and through what individuals do and involves efforts to discipline individual bodies for collective purposes. An obvious example of this is the way the state takes an interest in diet, healthy eating and not smoking. But any responsible parent does that for a child. So it is no exaggeration to say that our bodies are in part socially constructed.

Society has been involved in the way we look, not just as contrived appearance, obviously in dress, but even in physique. Just as human beings collectively have turned nature into distinctive landscapes so they have shaped their bodies. There are farmers and gardeners. There are nutritionists and body-builders too.

This awareness of individuality has been heightened because globalisation has diminished the hold of the nation-state on personal identity. This therefore heightens our understanding of the social basis of differences between people. The special nature of human social relations, of culture and of biology taken together all contribute to the distinctively human experience of personal uniqueness. Each one of us is bound to handle it in our own way.

Identity

If we recount history as a grand narrative of peoples and their achievements, as Herodotus began it (see p. 151), then your place and my place in this story as individuals is infinitesimally small. Yet it appears to matter to other people where we belong in it. Most people we meet will try to place us in a country and having a nationality. This is a main aspect of what we refer to when we talk about 'identity'.

For a sociologist the key fact is that it is other people who do the placing. They do it by finding a place for us in frames of reference which are widely shared, where outsiders and insiders regularly agree who belongs where at any one time. But belonging to a people, being from a country, is not straightforward because over time they move. Identity depends on your biography, the way you and others tell it and who you are with, and then it depends also on the grand narrative of peoples and countries.

After the Berlin Wall fell in 1989, and with the collapse of the Soviet Union, it became possible for people who had been Soviet citizens but long identified with Germany, and had been registered by the Soviets as of German nationality, to travel to Germany. For them it was a return 'home', though they had never lived there and it was several generations since their forebears had settled in Russia. The 'homecoming' proved a terrible shock. Germany was not a bit what they had expected and many became very unhappy.

International political changes leave their impressions on society and in turn on personal identity. But identities also live on and we may strive to retain an identity. The unification of Germany has not removed the identities acquired after its division in 1945. Eight years after reunification Germans still talk of each other as 'Ossies' and 'Wessies', and often employ stereotypes of the two in accounting for differences between people resident in the east and west of Germany.

'Ossies' and 'Wessies', 'Americans' and 'Chinese', 'Blacks' and 'Whites', 'Europeans' and 'Asians', 'Jews' and 'Aryans' are typical identity terms. They reek of history and come loaded with associations. Edward Said has pointed to the way Western self-images required the East to represent a negative counterpart as irrational and unreliable, as 'oriental'.[35] The politics of identity revolves around the power differentials which create these stereotypes. In the most generalised form they simply create 'the other'; simply the rest of humankind who fail to share the characteristics of one's chosen people.

The universal prevalence of these identity terms results from the reality of group membership. We can generalise from national identity and see this as true for all groups, men and women, old and young, beggars and rich people. We recognised earlier that relationships exist not just between particular people, but between types from which individual instances may diverge considerably. We have general ideas of what to expect of people whom we judge to be young, male, American and rich.

Very often this universal phenomenon of human society has been equated with prejudice in a negative sense. Sociologists find it more useful to speak in terms of 'typifications' rather than prejudice, which exists where a person refuses to recognise the reality of individual differences and allows the typification to distort their judgement. So it is prejudice if we don't recognise that this particular rich young American man is genuinely concerned to give service in poor countries.

But typifications may themselves be distortions, negatively or positively. We might be surprised to find that in fact rich young Americans generally want to serve, but we shouldn't assume either that this has anything to do with them being young, rich or American. Sociologists are not immune to prejudice themselves; their own special brand is the tendency to assume that individual characteristics are the product of group membership. It has to be an open issue. Assuming that individuals are entirely shaped by society and culture is what one sociologist has called the 'over-socialized conception of man'.[36]

No one can be sure how long a contemporary recognisable complex identity as, say, a sane, assertive, liberal, feminist, British working mother is here to stay. A considerable effort is involved on the part of those who hold it. I like the expression 'personal Odyssey' for the mix of striving, fate and grand narrative which make up the contemporary biography. It suggests that we can see the understanding of the struggle for identity as central to human experience even in the epics of Homer. The contemporary experience shares in the universal potential of humankind.

Trust

The negotiation of identity is the counterpart of the flux of boundaries. Given people's capacity to opt in or out, there is a permanent uncertainty about who is friend or foe, or whether the group exists or not. In contemporary sociology this has become an important theme. Uncertainty about the existence of society is often called 'ontological insecurity', a lack of confidence in surrounding reality, which is a more fundamental insecurity than that produced by lack of employment or health, which are often seen as the narrow area of 'social security'.

There are many who would argue that ontological insecurity has increased in contemporary society for many reasons, including the impact of mass media, migration and global markets. This is the background to the persistent call for a return to community where people know where they stand, which is expected to be much more than simply a welfare provider but rather a frame for social relations.

Yet revived community, potent though it may be as a slogan in political programmes, is not the only way in which human beings produce secure society. For community emphasises bonds which exclude as much as include. Social relations on the other hand cross boundaries as much as they constitute them. Anyone who travels makes assumptions about social relations in general and not just those within groups.

The counterpart to the theme of ontological insecurity is the one of trust – namely, our reliance on assumptions such as: strangers are generally friendly rather than hostile; it pays traders to be honest; my enemy doesn't want a destructive fight any more than I do. Of course these assumptions may turn out to be wrong, but if we don't adopt them then we avoid strangers, stop business and wage no-holds-barred conflict. There is therefore a general bias in social life towards benign trust, although without any guarantees.

Benign trust is a less obvious form of social integration than co-operation and it puts less emphasis on boundaries between social groups. Its minimal form is live and let live, its strongest is the assumption that others will regard your welfare in the same way as their own. Halfway is the idea that the other person has an interest in keeping their word. This is the basis of markets.

In the human social world where we don't know everyone in our group, and where anyone can enter or leave, and where we can't therefore be sure who is friend or enemy, the most basic relations we have are those of benign trust in the generalised other, just anyone, not anyone in particular. On its basis we can contemplate the possibilities of co-operation, of accords with our enemies and the luxury of competition in pursuit of common objectives.

In an older community-based theory of social integration its norms were held to be the basis of personal responsibility and loyalty to the group – the basis of morality. The loss of group norms was seen as 'anomie', with the danger of lapse into chaos. This assertion was a counter to idealist views of universal moralities, and indeed a boost for the tolerance of different cultures. But it gave the impression that sociology, and later anthropology, had to focus on the study of local cultures in order to counter the imbalance of abstract philosophies of humanity.

It disregarded the known fact of social interaction across boundaries and the very assumptions involved in travelling in foreign cultures even to study them: Bacon's courtesy to strangers.[37] But it would be blind optimism to imagine that trust alone will resolve conflict or bring peace and goodwill between people. There is evidence enough that relations between people are also driven by greed and the thirst for power.

On the other hand there is no evidence that a programme to return to communities without cleavage will diminish those drives, and considerable recent evidence to the contrary. It is in the institutions of the great society where we have to look to reduce the chances of carnage and degradation.

Chapter 4

Social
Institutions

From functions to practices

Institutions in practice

Sociology makes its most direct contribution to public life in its analysis of social institutions. This is because institutions normally work with public knowledge and support, and in our time draw on such wide expertise. As we saw in Chapter 1, social institutions involve standardised practices. They are widespread activities following norms about how things ought to be done. Norms are rules which are shared among a number of people who make an effort to ensure they are observed, especially through sanctions exerted on each other, these varying from mild disapproval to death. When norms are flouted then sociologists talk of deviance, without conveying their personal approval or disapproval of either norms or deviant acts.

Institutions are observed across collectivities and associations. They are social in that they contribute to collective life and receive widespread support even if

it is only a minority of individuals who derive the benefits. Contracts, lotteries, elections, mourning, holidays, taxation are examples of institutions from different spheres of life whose existence depends on their being recognised even by those who are bystanders, or by participants who do not benefit, as well as by those who do.

Institutions may develop around any area of human activity. For the ancient Egyptians health and the body were central concerns. In consequence they had specialist doctors for every part of the body, and specialists for embalming because it was so valued in that culture.[1] The development of institutions to this degree of specialisation is not then a result of modernity, but of any large-scale civilisation.

With most institutions their agents are in the first place concerned with outputs and results, not social relations. For instance healthcare institutions deliver treatment, and practitioners of them are expected to have this as their main concern. All institutions seek to deliver goods or services of one kind or other, valued products in the broadest sense, such as movies, fast food, legal judgements, sporting triumphs, last rites or election victories. This is even true of institutions which know no boundaries and are open to any individual. Think of the benefits expected from sending Christmas cards, though this is an institution in which the maintenance of social relations is a prime concern.

Because of the priority of the product or outcome, the social relations involved in maintaining an institution are often hidden from view. This is true even when institutions are embedded in collectivities like schools, factories or hospitals. Sociology brings them to the surface in a way which is variously called critical, demystifying or trouble-making, depending on your point of view.

Thus if sociologists point out that middle-class people get a better deal from healthcare institutions than poor people, the middle class may feel uncomfortable. But the deliverers of treatment, the medical professions, may be even more upset, for they are dedicated to providing the best practice regardless of the class of the patient. Ultimately, as we infer from our theory chapter, it flouts equality, a principle underlying medical ethics and a measurement standard for sociological research.

Not that the declared purposes of institutions are necessarily the ones which prevail. A frequent sociological finding is that the social relations of those who serve them often operate against the purposes of institutions. Bribery in business, racism within policing, sexism in employment are so widespread in many parts of the world that they also may be seen as institutionalised. This is in spite of the fact that governments as well as the collectivities concerned may try to root them out.

Even then institutions which run counter to state or employer policies and objectives are not necessarily against the public interest. Peter Blau's research on officials in a tax agency showed that they made a common practice of not reporting the offer of bribes, not because they accepted them but because their refusal of them put the person who made the offer in a false position and bound to be co-operative thereafter. Yet the official was breaking rules in not reporting the offer. The latent function of the officials' practice was to make the work of the tax agency run more smoothly.[2]

Latency, the features of social relations which hide behind public or official presentation, has always been a central focus for socio-logical fieldwork. The main contributions sociologists have made to industrial relations have been to show how people in the workplace really work rather than to provide schemes for the ideal organisation. The underlying social relations often used to be called 'informal organ-isation', but this downplays their importance. Norms set by workers may be far stronger influences on output than the paper targets set by management. Indeed the old saying that something may work in theory but not in practice is almost an axiom for sociology.

Not all institutions are for the public benefit, and inequality and cleavage are as evident in institutions as they are in collectivities. It was Sumner, author of the classic comparative study in this field, *Folkways*,[3] who pointed to the universality of ethnocentrism, the insti-tutional preference for people of your own country. Throughout the world equal opportunities legislation, often backed up by the idea of universal human rights, seeks to rectify this. But there is a deep tension here. The citizenship institutionalised in the modern nation-state is ethnocentric in principle: nationals get preference.

Institutions do not have to be centrally controlled, merely involve standardised expectations of how people will and ought to behave. But the state has a special relation to institutions and serves to shape them through law and coercion. Institutions to regulate gender and ethnic relations and the age of adulthood are obvious areas where the state is involved and seeks to govern the ambiguities and conflicts which arise out of changing social relations.

Even though new global authorities are developing, the nation-state is still the apex of institution building in the world today. But the vast majority of institutionalised practices in social relations are everyday and informally regulated, expressed as manners and etiquette, closely related to status, respect and dignity. In this way morals (like sexual fidelity), manners (like shaking hands), and fads (like body piercing), are weak forms of institution, permitting a great deal of divergence but none the less exerting some pressure on individuals to conform.

In most of these cases there are no specialists, but even so the practice supposedly delivers benefits to those who engage in it. However, self-interest is an inadequate explanation on its own for the existence of institutions, precisely because there are pressures to conform, because deviance is widespread, and there are agencies of social control.

Institutional theory

Broadly there are three general theories to account for the emergence and existence of institutions. Unfortunately the first two both get called 'functionalist', but at bottom they are very different even though many attempts have been made to combine them. One, which has been associated particularly with Talcott Parsons, argues that institutions serve the continued existence of society because it would fall into chaos without them.[4] The other, effectively expressed by the anthropologist Bronislaw Malinowski, says they grow up around and serve human needs.[5] To distinguish them we will call the former the functionalist and the latter the need theory. The third sees them as the outcome of rational choice among people seeking best outcomes in their activities.

The functionalist theory of institutions has lost much credibility since the 1950s when it was in its heyday, mainly because too much was claimed for it. Basically the total array of activities in a society were thought of as being organised around institutional areas or sectors such as the economy, education, religion, politics, each of which contributed to the survival of society as a whole and in which people had to be motivated to work. Rewards, in terms of income and status, followed performance as a result, and activities which did not contribute to the common good were correspondingly regarded as deviant.

There was a strong reaction against this theory in the 1960s. It was attacked particularly for being an ideological account, which neglected coercion and conflict and overlooked class interests. It saw needs as the product of and serving society, rather than simply developed in and through it. The corollary was the 'over-socialised conception of man' we noticed in Chapter 3.[6] From a standpoint today the assumptions that culture serves society and that society is to be equated with nation-state society are most questionable. Overall the problem with functionalism is that the theory subordinates human activities to the collectivity instead of seeing them as people's engagement with reality or the world.

Certainly there are institutions which are key to the survival of particular collectivities. Without money and credit the banking system collapses, without the mass and the Pope the Catholic Church would not survive, and the monarchy may well be indispensable to Britain (though not to Scotland, Wales or England). But the point is that none of these collectivities has any permanent guarantee of existence and society in general would get on without them, but in a different way.

The need theory of institutions makes society exist for them rather than the reverse. It asserts that it is through society that human beings develop institutionalised practices which enhance the development of human powers, creative expression, fulfilment of desire and satisfaction of need. The need theory is right to this extent. Society is the base and vehicle for these, not their goal. Certainly if key institutions concerned with reproduction, nutrition, shelter and security were to collapse then society would too, but this is because society can only exist if the basic needs of the species are met.

The problem with this theory is that it has difficulty in interpreting the cultural diversity of institutions if their origin is traced back to general human needs. It also appears to leave society as entirely open-ended as a solution to needs when we know that there are a restricted number of options and of these some are universal, for instance norms and authority. The need theory's solution is somewhat lame here, effectively saying society is itself a need, the answer of Aristotle and Marx: human beings are 'social animals'.

This is where rational choice theory applied to institutions makes a precise intervention to help in explaining their existence. It provides both for trial and error and rational calculation as strategies to deal with the circumstances in which individuals find themselves, and treats collective solutions as one way to reduce uncertainty. It allows for the evolution of the variety of institutions as passing solutions to perennial problems under different environmental conditions.

It may exaggerate calculation compared with drives, desires and force, all contributing to human power, and in particular the power of some over others. But in a form known as 'neo-institutionalism' this theory challenges a lot of older sociology. Paradoxically beginning with individual choice it has been more successful in demonstrating the necessity for the existence of society than any theory previously. It does this by showing that if you begin with the unrealistic fiction that only individuals and their purposes exist you finish up with showing the necessity for society, not a war of all against all. Indeed the most important statement of this theory, James S. Coleman's, argues that a set of individuals pursuing their own purposes will demand norms and realise them in their own actions.[7]

Some might think that there is little point in assuming the opposite of the truth and then proving it wrong. However, the thrust of the old modern theory of society, especially that kind which developed in economics, was to suggest that individuals following their own purposes were likely to destroy the foundations of society, the nightmare of William Golding's novel *Lord of the Flies* where the society of children isolated on an island descends into chaos. The only solution to this in older social theory was that made famous by Thomas Hobbes with his Leviathan, a sovereign power imposing order, or in the modern functionalism of Talcott Parsons which assumes a prior consensus on values. Old social theory oscillated between absolute power or consensus as solutions, neither of which corresponded to the facts of society as sociologists described them.

What Coleman's argument shows is that there is no reason to fear the break-up of society through ever-increasing individualisation, though he diminishes the effect of his argument by insisting on parental imposition of norms on children. Theoretically, as opposed to Golding, children too will develop norms, and this corresponds to much of their play behaviour. The big problem is to explain the outbreaks of violence which are not to anyone's benefit. What, however, one can observe about the norms which each generation develops is that they can frequently run counter to those of a previous generation and that in itself accounts for much of the fear of the breakdown of society.

None of the three theories is adequate on its own to explain the nature, standardisation and variety of institutions. Rational choice theory explains both the variety and standardisation of institutions but not the nature of the needs they fulfil; needs theory cannot explain either variety or standardisation; and functionalist theory explains standardisation but not variety. On the face of it a merger of the three would provide an all-round view.

In fact this does not occur because the answers we give to the questions of how institutions fulfil needs, how they are standardised and how their variety arises are different when considered separately than they would be taken together. We are born into an ongoing society, in which human needs are evolving all the time and where standardisation is constantly being reconstituted on new bases. The interaction effects result in a constant dynamic, a cycle of change and retrenchment, on which there have been reflections throughout history.

The theory of institutions cannot be adequate to this change so long as it treats education, law, religion, etc. as institutions only; that is, standardised practices. But education is more than a standardised practice. It is an individual and shared experience of the world, an activity which always transcends and challenges norms. The theory of practice and institutions can be misleadingly conservative if it does not allow for development of experience and the acquisition of new powers and understandings.

So long as basic human needs are met, the limits to the kinds of institution which may develop are human capacities, material resources, culture, technical development and social relations. But this permits a vast range. Journalism and computing for instance belong to the modern (and postmodern) world, embalming and body piercing on the other hand are widely dispersed historically, but infrequently occurring. Cooking and poetry are universal. But the development of the powers and potential of human beings always takes us beyond the confines of society.

The sociology of institutions is an important point of intersection between sociology and all the disciplines which deal with specialised skills and capacities. Medicine, sport, education, law, art, social work look to sociology for an understanding of society. But while the sociology of each of these is rewarding and has a large literature and fund of research, we would need something encyclopaedic to cover them.

Instead we will consider five sectors of experience which pervade every institution and collectivity. They challenge every society because they are life-spheres for us all. They are areas of activity within which institutions grow but where we also confront standardised practices through our active engagement in the world and in the development of our own unique capacities. They are state, work, environment, culture and the person.

In each case I will stress the challenge which current changes in these life-spheres pose to old conceptions of their functions for society. At the end we will consider the question of whether there is a distinct sphere for society or whether it is simply the basis for any and all life-spheres.

Changes in the life-spheres

Beyond state societies

We begin with the sphere which dominates institutions in modern societies and at the same time has the most fraught relations with society. Gains for the state appear often as loss to society, and scholars and radicals of all kinds have speculated on the possibilities of society without the state, or at least with only a minimal state.

From the viewpoint of institutional leaders and practitioners, however, their prime interest in society is that it should be predictable.

They want to ensure steady flows of recruits, respect for their work and status in society. Their interest in culture, too, is in guarantees for their rights to practice in and control their sector and assert its claims for public attention against others. For all of these things they look to the state. It is the autonomy of social relations which makes social control a generic issue for all institutional work. It is the autonomy of culture which leads practitioners to enlist the state's help in asserting professional monopoly.

There is then a common interest among those who run institutions in enhancing the predictability of society. They exercise 'hegemony' – as the Italian Marxist theorist Antonio Gramsci developed the idea, borrowing from both Marx and Weber – as power operating through ideas and everyday practices.[8] They work with the state for ways of enforcing compliance with their own requirements. The very name 'state' conveys its character as the institution to secure institutions, to give them a fixed and settled base. To do this the state engages in the regulation and control of social relations, and because these are inherently fluid we encounter the fraught issue of the relations of state and society.

There is an oppositional ideology as counterpart to dominant ideology, namely the conviction that institutions can be made to serve those who work in them. This is the inspiration of workers' collectives. But this only repeats the basic error of those leaders who seek to make institutions work for their own advantage. Factories don't exist to serve the needs of those who work in them, and there never would have been factories if that was their function. They don't even in the first instance exist to serve their owners and managers. They produce for the needs of customers.

As we discussed earlier in our account of human collectivities, the social relations of the factory are the core of a set of practices, technology, plant, buildings, finance. Their output supplies goods for people through the mechanism of the market, not for society, even less for the state (unless it happens also to be the customer). For this reason Karl Marx would have nothing to do with socialist schemes of workers' control. Instead he looked forward to a time when the disappearance of class division would mean that institutions could serve general human needs.

Both in the United States and Britain attempts have been made in the last two decades to take the heat out of the issue of the control of institutions with the notion of the stakeholder, recognising the wide diversity of sectional interests involved in any institution and therefore of claims on its outputs. This recognises a wider constellation of social relations than even owners, workers and customers, and can provide a forum for the innocent bystander – the victim of environmental degradation for instance.

Stakeholding is not a panacea. There is a danger that handing over institutions to an identified set of stakeholders will damage openended provision of needs. But environmental damage appears a clear-cut case of market failure. Fulfilment of the needs of some can damage the interests of the many and some other mechanism is needed for institutional control. At the moment the central state remains as the only effective arbiter, lobbied by watchdog groups of all kinds.

When sociologists study any institutional area they look to the social origins, status and class position of its agents, the kinds of people it serves and how its services are distributed among them, to social relations involved in institutional practices, and the consequences of the institution for the structuration of the wider society. As we have stressed all this is fluid and the participants look to the state to deliver control. But the state as this controller of institutions is in turn subject to the same range of influences from society. This, then, is the old question of 'Who guards the guardians?'

The regulation of society by the state has become a highly technical matter, involving the employment of specialised officials and professionals from many fields, from law to public health, weapons technology to computing, social work to education. For the modern world this technical apparatus of the state, summed up in the word 'bureaucracy', has come to be central to it.

But before modern bureaucracy, going back to Aristotle, the issue of who ruled and how rulers were selected was always regarded as fundamental. This was the basis of the classic theory of the differences between democracy, oligarchy and monarchy. The quality of the rulers determined the character of the state. The modern state's peculiarity was that it generated a new social class, the bureaucrats, its servants who became its rulers. In the modern nation-state the state begins to generate its own kind of control society and ceases to be simply a mechanism for ruling society.

These contrasts over time between different kinds of state mean we have to be careful to find a concept of state which has the widest possible relevance. The traditional classification of types of state set them in the wider context of society. Therefore the state exists in a special kind of relation to social relations, sometimes as a restriction on them, sometimes as an extension of their possibilities. Your evening social party is not a state event, but the state may intervene if your sound system is too loud. Your political party activity, however, is only possible because the state exists.

So what is the state? The state exists – and here follows a definition – *in the organisation of practices of enforcement of a public interest or good by some people on others*. This is enormously broad. But note it is a lot narrower than our idea of society, which also includes social relations in private, unorganised, unenforced and just plain matters of taste and preference.

But our definition also brings to view the tensions between state and society. Just how far can the state extend its interest in private activities? Does it extend to the consenting activities of sado-masochistic adults in private? A recent judgement of the European Court of Justice declared that it did when it rejected an appeal against the verdict of a British court which had declared it was illegal for a man to agree to his penis being pierced.

In other words the boundaries between those social activities which are required, forbidden or simply permitted by the state are always being tested in practice and are never firm. They vary between one nation-state and another and sometimes the practices of states in general will undermine those of a particular state. After holding out for a long time Ireland has finally come into line with other nation-states in making divorce legal. Both of these examples raise the question of which state: Britain or Europe; Ireland or the state in general? Our definition leaves this open, as it has to, because the success of the claim to be a state is one which will depend on power and historic rights which are always contestable. Being a state depends on the power to assert rights and to be recognised as a state by other states. This is where the nation-state has come to be regarded as the only real state and the test of statehood has been recognition by other nation-states.

But if we go back to our definition we can see it says nothing about nation. It allows for the fact that statehood exists both at local and international levels. The nation-state claims to be the source of the power at both those levels. But even that is open to contest. We have talked about rights and their assertion. People, movements and organisations are not always prepared to allow nation-states to be the sole arbiter of these. They resist tyrannical states, and since 1945 a complex law of human rights has been established on a global scale.

On our definition the state may exist both below the nation-state level in citizen initiatives and in the activities of transnational non-governmental organisations which seek to save the planet or end state torture. Older sociological definitions of the state effectively represented the claims of the nation-state of the day. The classic definition of the nation-state by Max Weber was of an organisation which laid successful claim to the monopoly of legitimate physical force in a territorial area.[9] His formulation captured the essence of the state in the period of the imperialistic nationalism at the beginning of the twentieth century. But the world has changed.

We can see that the routine administration of the state in the late twentieth century is based on more than the monopoly of legitimate violence. Now, it depends equally on technical systems and a sense of justice, which limit the adequacy, scope and legitimacy of violence in the service of the state. The claim to monopoly of violence was another way of expressing the idea of sovereignty, that no other body could claim jurisdiction. In reality that was never completely realised and in today's world of federal and overlapping authorities it is not always clear who can detain whom or confiscate which property in which area. The pursuit of war criminals outside their own nation-state is a prime example of a state beyond the nation-state.

A sociological definition of the state is bound to take account of shifting new realities and the inherent tension which results between society and the state. It is crucial to understand that the state does not create society. It is not even the only source of regularity and predictability in human affairs. A huge amount of this is the product of manners and customs without a coercive apparatus. Relations in private can be just as ordered as public ones. Interpersonal relations even between strangers may proceed smoothly without state intervention. But there will always be an argument about what would happen if the state were not there as some guarantee.

This is true of all those institutions where the main concern is not with the regulation of social relations but with outputs in the wider world, with the production both of material and ideal objects. Work is central to all of them and if we attend to the sociology of work we have a lead on the preconditions for the survival of any institution.

Work for human needs

Work has always been the life-sphere where visionaries have thought it possible for social relations to develop beyond the control of the state. It is the modern counterweight to the nation-state for radical thinkers. This was true for the political economy of Adam Smith and the historical materialism of Karl Marx. Both believed the source of value was work. For Smith the exchange of products depended on the prior social division of labour. For Marx production depended on the social relations of capital and labour. Each minimised the role of the state, to be the watchdog in the first case and to be the instrument of class rule in the second. Both believed that in work society revealed its nature: as exchange for Smith, as co-operation for Marx.

For both work placed human beings in relation to nature, both their own and what was outside them. Any collective activity, whether in exchange or co-operation, therefore served to realise human nature. Political economy, later to be called economics, began as a modern theory of society distinct from both Christian and classical theories. It came to be known as the theory of civil society.

Ironically the autonomy of the institutional order which arose from economic activity was precisely what challenged the state authorities in the nineteenth century. Theorists of civil society like Adam Ferguson knew full well it was intrinsically a class society. The division of labour meant the growth of distinct occupations and professions which were independent of the state. As Marx observed, it was their growth which led to the overthrow of the old regime in

France in the French Revolution of 1789. The threat which the new class of workers posed to the state and bourgeois order in the nineteenth century was what prompted the Western response of welfare statism or corporatism. The state was meant to represent society and institutions were shaped to serve it. In the Soviet Union and its satellites this dominance of the state was even more acute as supposedly the Russian Revolution resulted in the triumph of the mass of the people.

The twentieth century was dominated by the question of how far the state should control the social organisation of work, whether totally as in communism or fascism or partially as in the Western parliamentary democracies. Even in the latter state control has grown to the point where its share of gross national product, the total sum of goods and services, is between 40 and 60 per cent

This is an upside-down world compared with the time of Smith or Marx, where state now equates with society and what was society has become 'private' and even anti-social. The very rich place their funds in enclaves outside nation-state boundaries so that a recent estimate suggests a third of their wealth is in accounts on small islands.[10] Ironically the very term 'society' remains current as the high society, the interpersonal social relations, of the owners of wealth.

In the workplace where employers and workers confronted each other the state sought to damp down the ever-likely prospect of disruption to production. The mechanisms which were devised to contain disputes and provide for partnership, arbitration or trade union representation have been called the institutionalisation of conflict, to reflect the assumption on both sides that a degree of conflict was inevitable and had to be managed.

The modern battle about class interests and the state was the focus both of inter-state conflict in the Cold War and ideological conflict between left and right within nation-states. The two conflicts reinforced each other in the sense that the contestants within the state sought support from the other side. In a sense, the Cold War explained the close interest of the Western state in what were known as industrial relations and promoted state involvement. At the same time it drew attention away from the deep transformation of social relations which were taking place in work.

New service occupations and new technology, the informatisation of work, the decline of the old smokestack industries, the entry into what is sometimes called the post-Fordist era, has seen a decline in the opposition between the people, understood as workers, and the state. Economics itself has developed the new institutionalism which emphasises practices in the firm and the wider culture. It reflects the shift in the balance of power in society away from the state and towards the institutions of work. In the new working practices of the contemporary economy types of social relations develop which make the older state institutionalisation of class relations in the workplace irrelevant.

This is where the idea of stakeholding is relevant as it seeks to fill the place vacated by old-style industrial relations. The purposes of work in serving and fulfilling human needs can once again find a central place among human values, not as the functional requirement of nation-state society nor even just of the particular organisation. Work is involved in every institutional area, production often of very intangible things, for which skill and expertise is necessary. It relates people to the world in the broadest sense, to their physical and cultural environment, but also equally as well to other people. Only when policy-makers, employers and managers recognise that people are involved in social relations *beyond* the scope of their planning has society achieved its proper place in relation to the state and economy.

Workers have families, volunteers have jobs, donors have social status, political party members live in communities, and political leaders have ethnicity. These are not freely disposable involvements. They go to constitute the person's social identity, represent opposition to schemes as well as the source of movements which no one controls. They are, in short, the facticity, the day-to-day reality of society.

These social relations also provide the basis for economic activity. Max Weber's famous thesis was that capitalism obtained a big boost from Protestant religious ideas on work.[11] Often Weber's thesis has been used to illustrate the importance of ideas. But it also shows that work predates capitalism. It has to. It is universal.

Work involves effort, a striving to make some part of the world meet what you and other people need or want. It engages with an environment, including other people too. It regularly uses tools and technology, but they are not essential to the idea of work. In this sense we know of no time in history where people haven't worked.

My definition of work is controversial. For it runs counter to another widespread modern myth. This is the idea that work was somehow brought to new peaks of intensity, if it was not actually invented, in the modern period in the West. People world-wide, outside the modern West, were held to be either lazy or so set in traditional ways of doing things that they could do them unthinkingly and without effort.

Unfortunately professional sociologists have tended to use Weber's theory to reinforce the self-image of modernity that only under Western capitalism did people begin to do real work. Students of pre-modern societies have long recognised that work is intrinsic to the human condition. As Marshall Sahlins has put it 'no anthropologist today would concede the truth of the imperialist ideology that the natives are congenitally lazy'.[12] Another anthropologist, Raymond Firth, explicitly challenged the myth when he pointed to the way the New Zealand Maoris made great use of proverbs to spur on the lazy.[13]

We can even take an example from the present day of a pre-literate people who have become a byword for the ravages of Western civilisation on ancient cultures. Colin Turnbull's studies of the Ik people of northern Uganda depict a disintegrating society in which selfishness is the main survival strategy. Yet when the Ik worked on making spears it was done with great care and precision and showed fine craftsmanship. It was here too that a minimal degree of co-operation was achieved.[14] But there is also the literary evidence. The ancient Israelites' book of Exodus commanded them to labour for six days.

The fact that work has been an intrinsic aspect of the human condition encouraged Thorstein Veblen, the great exposer of the idleness and waste of what he called the leisure class, to write of 'the instinct of workmanship'.[15] The idea that there are inherent deep satisfactions in work also underpinned Karl Marx's account of alienated labour under capitalism. It prompted him to dream of times past and to come when work might once again express our true nature. But it was the realities Marx exposed of work in the modern period, grinding labour in the workplace, which came to dominate views of the nature of work. Weber's picture of the joyless self-discipline of the Puritan went to reinforce these views. He depicted the motives which could sustain such a process. No wonder his image of the 'iron cage' seemed to fit the idea of modern work.

Of all the civilisations which have been the victim of Western misinterpretation of motivation to work none has been more unjustly treated than China. It became a modernist cliché, from the seventeenth century onwards, that this was a society in which culture had stood still and no one would work to improve their condition. Only in the last decade has it dawned on the West that it has seriously misunderstood the culture of Eastern countries. The main reason for this late realisation was the economic success in the 1980s – first of the Japanese and then of other countries, the Eastern Tigers, bordering China – which has challenged the world economic dominance of North America and Europe.

For Asian countries owe nothing to a Protestant ethic. They have common cultural roots in the ethic of Confucius, the Chinese sage, adviser to rulers, who lived 500 years before Christ. We can read to this day what he said about work:

> Tzu-lu asked about government. The Master said, 'Encourage the people to work hard by setting an example yourself.' Tzu-lu asked for more. The Master said, 'Do not allow your efforts to slacken'.[16]

Of the great world ethical systems the Confucian was distinctive for seeking to bind study and skills together. In the notion of competence in rituals there was a very real demonstration of the importance of combining the two. For Confucius the learning of the scholar could only be worth while when expressed as useful skills. Let us be hard-headed about this. The motives of the Chinese scholars were not disinterested. Their society was overwhelmingly a two- or at best three-class one, of peasants, landlords and officials. The officials undertook a long and arduous education. They sought to persuade owners and peasantry of its worth and to bind the classes together in one harmonious whole. In that sense the status order of the society governed supply of positions which were open to competition and motivated to work. In fact Western economists have acknowledged how important this basic sociological factor is for the economy. Where work is devoted to obtaining positional goods then there isn't much growth.[17]

One of the greatest transformations of the present time is that there is a new combination of mental and manual activity. This operates not, as in ancient civilisations, as co-operation between classes, but in the transformation of the work of the masses. The result is that the division of older societies between mental and manual labour has broken down. The main theme in the analysis of work in society in the old modern period was first the division of labour between different specialised occupations and then later class conflict rather than co-operation.

Now the old dividing lines are blurred. The farmer and the gardener today will also have their paper qualifications, reflecting periods working for examinations as well as with soil. This also involves the development of new kinds of work and the decline of the massive concentrations of workers in the smokestack production plants of the modern age. Service jobs replace those in manufacturing. The computer-aided graphic designer replaces the artist, the draughtsman and the toolmaker simultaneously and never comes near a factory gate. We see it in the new agriculture where the lone farmer may engage in capital intensive farming with no employees.

Such a person may also be working independently on his or her own behalf. It is not 'political correctness' to speak of 'his or her' in this context. The gender divides in occupations are increasingly blurred, even as old boundaries between occupations disappear. Yet the sex of a person is as relevant as ever for chances of long-term success. How many students are female? About 50 per cent. How many professors are female? About 4 per cent. So what's going on? Where did all the women go?

The academic world is no different from many others – medicine, management, law among them – in that advantages accrue to those who can work continuously in the one sphere. Women take time out of those spheres, not to be idle but to do something very demanding of time, care and skill; namely, rearing children.

Still, overwhelmingly, world-wide, childcare is thought of as women's work, and as more and more women are drawn into working for money their disadvantaged position in the marketplace becomes more obvious. Not surprisingly women are more and more reluctant to have children as it is obvious that they lose earning chances as a result.

Public responses to this situation in the West range from advocating a return to home and hearth for women to campaigning for equal rights for men to care for children, or for wages for housework. These strategies are taken up by different people as personal lifestyle options – 'traditional woman' or 'new man' – and contribute to the continuing development of diversity of household and family arrangements.

For most people there are now trade-offs to be made between domestic labour and work for money. With couples there are decisions to be made about who does more unpaid work and who does paid work, since there are no longer straightforward gender divisions for work at home or in a workplace. 'Going out to work' is not the only way to earn a living. The woman writer, potter, or physiotherapist may work for money at home while her partner looks after their children. These are not easy arrangements to make and Ray Pahl has shown how the domestic division of labour has become an arena for interpersonal conflict as well as for personal development beyond the old gender boundaries.[18]

When we put all these contemporary changes together we can see that in some ways work has recovered the place it had before the modern age – necessary for life, a way of living, a source of effort and of satisfaction, with no guarantees in any respect. Contemporary work is insecure too, in a risky world, just as is pre-modern work in a very different environment. But our sense of continuity or return to a past ought also to alert us to what is really new. Hardly anywhere in the world anymore can people work to be self-sufficient and independent of a market for what they make and do.

After a period in which the main trend seemed to be towards the reduction of everyone to being unskilled labourers we have entered a time when personal capital has become fundamental to livelihood. That capital is to be of course counted in terms of savings, pensions and homeownership in part, then in terms of possessions, tools, and facilities. But more important than any of these is personal cultural capital: qualifications, skills acquired through education, training and experience. This is capital which can itself be acquired through work and is necessary for further work. It is the basis of what some sociologists call 'knowledge society'.[19] Paradoxically we are now more aware than ever of what we don't know, how far we are exposed to hazards knowledge has helped to create. We will consider knowledge society's counterpart, 'ignorance society', in the next chapter.

Environment as global risk

Sociologists have always been unsure about their relations with the human environment. They issue warnings to students at an early stage of their studies to avoid 'geographical determinism', which means trying to explain social facts from natural surroundings like Herodotus occasionally did: 'the natives are black because of the hot climate'.[20]

Émile Durkheim, the great French founder of professional sociology, wrote that 'it is not the land which explains man, it is man which explains the land'.[21] He was equally dismissive that climate might be a causal factor in suicide rates. He insisted that 'a social fact can only be explained by another social fact',[22] and in this way believed he could make sociology into an independent science.

But it is one thing to assert the distinct reality of society and quite another to treat it as immune to outside influence or indeed as the only source of change in the world. Human beings make their own history but not under conditions of their own choosing; this was Karl Marx's more modest formulation of humankind's fate. But in terms of Marx's own materialism he too overstated the independence of humankind from wider reality. If we emphasise society as a human construction, nature is a constituent and not simply on the outside. Society, human social relations, exist in and through material objects, either natural or manufactured. Is technology human or non-human? The answer is that, as an extension of social relations, it is both. In considering collectivities in Chapter 1 we saw the motor vehicle literally as a feature of society in motion.

This complexity of relations between human beings, society and the natural world is only an intensification of the intricate relations between any species and its environment, which prompted the German biologist Ernest Haeckel to invent the term 'ecology' in 1868 to refer to its study. Since then there have been a variety of attempts to develop ecological approaches to human existence. American sociologists in Chicago developed human ecology mainly as the study of the unplanned concentration and distribution of human activities in different areas. The division of urban space between leafy suburb and downtown slum is an outcome of human activity, which determines relations between the dwellers of each area.

The early Chicago approach to the environment was not dissimilar to the Marxist approach to the economy. Each stressed the unplanned outcomes of human activities for the organisation of social relations. It was sociological in Durkheim's sense that 'man explains the land'. Even when resources were taken into account they became an aspect of an ecosystem sustaining a population. In the late twentieth century there has been a broad shift of opinion away from treating the environment as the inexhaustible storehouse for modern expansion. Rather than being self-sustaining, human activity can equally well be self-destructive by damaging the conditions for its own existence. Since the Brundtland Report of 1987[23] the idea of 'sustainable development' has become the watchword for a new politics of the environment.

Sociologists have assimilated the concerns of the environmental movement and turned to accounting for its sources of social support and its responses to the environment. The sociology of the environment becomes the sociology of environmentalism, the study of organisation for the environment.[24] There are some who might regard this as a retreat into navel gazing. Instead of being concerned directly with human impact on the environment, sociologists have come to study why people are concerned with it and how they organise themselves for it. This is a more modest project in many ways. But this refocusing on social relations entails a radical reassessment of humankind's place in nature.

For a start it refuses to assume that nature is under control. Nor does it assume a self-sustaining ecosystem. Rather, it points to human reactions to an environment which is unpredictable. It acknowledges that human activities have had effects on the environment, but the environment also strikes back. The consequences are dangerous and chaotic compared with the regularities of urban zoning.

Sociologists have come to emphasise that much social organisation is now concerned with the management of risk, and exposure to environmental hazards is one of the main forms of risk. The German sociologist Ulrich Beck has summed up contemporary social relations as risk society, a threatening image compared with older ideas of a modern affluent or welfare society but one which expresses today's widespread sense of personal insecurity.[25] In some ways this is reminiscent of non-modern societies. For 2,000 years the Chinese emperor was held to be responsible for warding off natural disaster and the provision of water and flood control, and emergency food supplies were key features of social organisation in imperial China.

The sociology of human relations with the environment means serious study of the exposures to risk and to the enjoyment of environmental benefits of different human groups. It takes organising for and in relation to the environment as a central theme. It equally recognises the historic transformation of the environment as an outcome of economic development. But unlike older approaches this new environmental sociology has no expectation that the transformed environment is any more controlled, benign or predictable than it has ever been. The threats are different however. There have been real changes and one of them is the enhancement of global risk.

There are broadly three kinds of environmental change which expose our species to global risk. The first is in the cumulative depletion and eventual exhaustion of resources which have world-wide use, as with carbon fuels. The second is the degradation and destruction of the conditions for human life as an effect of the aggregate of human activities. The destruction of the ozone layer and consequent global warming is an example. The third is the consequences of catastrophe which because of technological advance has global outreach. The Chernobyl nuclear reactor meltdown of 1986 was one such foretaste of possibilities in this respect.

None of these are willed outcomes of human activities and their impact is irregular. For that reason the environment is an unpredictable and impersonal force in contemporary world history, releasing events to which the human response is to organise on a global scale. We can speak of globalisation in this respect, not as some inevitable natural process but as an incremental human response to the challenge of the size and scale of the new risks which have arisen out of humankind's interaction with the environment.

The sociology of that response shows that there is no single strategy for dealing with global risk. 'Think globally, act locally', for years the slogan of Friends of the Earth, suggested a grass-roots popular movement, but Greenpeace has made its impact through professional organisation and use of the media. Additionally, both institutions of global governance in meetings like the Rio Earth Summit of 1992 and global capitalist interests have responded to environmental concerns.

Global risks cross frontiers and the awareness of this has forced sociology back to a direct concern with society beyond nation-state boundaries. In an older modern sociology the locatedness of social relations in particular places was taken for granted. Communities, cities and nation-states were all seen as territorial units and individuals took both their identity and roots from them. The territorial map of political divisions was also a map of society.

But social relations have never depended on fixity to place or proximity for their continuation. This is a variable feature of human society and contrary to many views there is no clear direction in history. Some societies have placed more emphasis on rootedness in a locality than others, and have also had different expectations of classes and groups. The European feudal lord or the Chinese official travelled from area to area, but the serf or peasant might be bound for a lifetime to one place.

Viking literature extols absence as the true test of a human relationship: 'love will be lost if you sit too long at a friend's fire.'[26] The saying 'absence makes the heart grow fonder' goes back to 1602.[27] So what some sociologists and geographers have called disembedding,[28] the abstraction of social relations and systems from particular places which new technology of communication and travel facilitates, is not so much new as the revival of consciousness that social relations occupy social space.

The geographer David Harvey has emphasised that the contemporary world involves time/space compression.[29] We don't have to stay in the same geographical location for long periods for people to rely on staying in touch with us. On the other hand staying in one place is no obstacle to world-wide communication. But this 'small world' effect is also a 'multiple worlds' experience. In any one place many scenes from different dramas are being enacted simultaneously.

This abstraction of social relations from particular places highlights the special features of human society. At the same time it makes geography a lot more interesting. For a start we can't read off social class and status from territorial location in the way urban zoning theory assumed. The new media of social relations, communications and information technology, the development of a single world financial market and corporations with global outreach, constitute the forces of economic globalisation. The inner cities, industrial areas and countryside in the West are undergoing multiple transformations which are not just the effect of the decline of industry. A multinational aerospace corporation may be assembling aircraft in an area where farmers are producing organic food for local needs.

But globalisation processes don't pull in one direction. Moreover, the consciousness of common risks in environmentalism and the new sense of global citizenship inspire new social movements. Campaigns for civil rights, of women or of children cross boundaries. This is globalisation from below. The nation-state in the past imposed a territorial frame on social relations which made it difficult to disentangle state, nation, society and place. Now the state finds it difficult to hold these together as people and organisations find their ties cross boundaries in multiple ways.

Any one place now presents to a greater or lesser degree a socioscape of ties with the wider world.[30] It is not that people in general are less dependent on each other or on places than they were. The interdependencies cross the globe in a new way and the places may be various and miles apart. We used to think of people building up a personal milieu of people, objects and territory which was localised in one place. Now that milieu may be extended to many places, or even in virtual reality.[31] In this respect our ability to travel is less important than our access to representations of distant places. We become cultural tourists as we stroll through the shopping mall or relax in front of a screen.

The autonomy of culture

In a famous definition of culture the nineteenth-century anthropologist E.B. Tylor proposed that culture is:

> that complex whole which includes knowledge, belief, art, morals, law, custom, and any other capabilities and habits acquired by man as a member of society.[32]

This doesn't leave much which is not either mentioned or implied. It speaks of society and, since it talks of capabilities and habits acquired in it, presumably will also include politics, economics, religion, and so on.

And yet there is a special slant to this definition. We may note it refers to a 'complex whole', to what is 'acquired in society' and so seems to allow that not all is acquired in society. 'Capabilities and habits' is not quite as comprehensive as might appear at first sight either. We have often spoken of social space, position and status. They are occupied by people to be sure, but are not exactly capabilities, more facilities or resources. So society and culture are not the same.

Another anthropologist writing in the middle of the twentieth century brings out the difference in this way. He calls society the 'aggregate set of social relations' and culture 'the content of those relations'.[33] Society then appears as a kind of container for culture. This distinction between form and content, with social relations being the form and culture the content, has a strategic place in the history of sociology. We may recall the Chicago School and Simmel, who was the most influential theorist at the beginning of the century for professional sociology, and he made it a central element of his work.

But form and content is a metaphor from geometry or art and can be misleading. Social relations are also learned and conducted within frames of meaning. We can just as easily say that language is the form and social relations the content. The most misleading direction this metaphor takes is to suggest that social relations must be to culture like the structure of a building is to its materials. Then we find that the boundaries of the one set the limits of the other. This is indeed is the thrust of nation-state ideology, which seeks to ensure closure of its borders to foreigners and to isolate its culture from foreign influences.

Simmel insisted usefully that form and content could vary independently of each other. So did Weber. He insisted that capitalist organisation could be associated with many different beliefs and motives. There is a direct line from this to contemporary management's concern for getting organisational culture right – which means the same organisation has different cultural possibilities.

Simmel and Weber stressed the diversity of culture and cultures and the widespread use of the concept. Later scholars have underwritten this. One study collected 160 definitions of culture from a variety of disciplines.[34] The separation of culture and society, and the generic nature of the issue of culture across disciplines, has resulted in a new discipline: cultural studies with many affinities and links with sociology. Thus cultural studies treats popular culture as equally worthy of academic study as elite culture and refuses to take sides on their worth.

Whereas at one time culture was thought of as the property of those with a privileged education, the new discipline particularly focuses on culture as a pervasive everyday thing, on television, fashion, advertising, consumer products, lifestyles. So the outlook and habits of a group of school rejects which Paul Willis studied in an English industrial town[35] are just as suitable for cultural studies as the topic Georgina Born took: how the musical avant-garde works around Pierre Boulez.[36]

For the general public the difference between cultural studies and sociology may not appear so important. But the background to the divide is complex and goes to the heart of some of the most important debates in Western intellectual history. In many respects it is the continuation of a nineteenth-century debate which raged between idealists and materialists, those who argued that ideas directed the course of history and those who asserted the prime importance of material forces. Professional sociology, with Weber a leader in this with his emphasis on religious ideas, struggled to settle the debate by giving both ideas and the material world a place in shaping society.

For the followers of Marx's historical materialism this made sociology itself an ideology, an expression of class interest. Academic disciplines were clearly also part of culture. So by the 1960s the debate had shifted to focus on the relation of intellectual life to capitalism and how it might serve or undermine those interests.

Effectively that very shift signalled the defeat of historical materialism. Evidently it did matter which ideas intellectuals promoted and Marxists were among the most ardent intellectuals. Post-colonial conditions after the withdrawal of Western states from direct control also forced recognition that new nationalisms rather than international solidarity asserted themselves on historical cultural and linguistic lines and not just on the territorial boundaries Western states left behind. It was not possible to attribute linguistic boundaries in new states to capitalism.

In the late twentieth century the nation, as much as class, has been the focus for the debate about culture. But this shifting base for culture – class or nation – in itself emphasises its independence from any given set of social relations. So we have the paradox that the most influential figures within cultural studies, who treat culture as a topic for independent study, have been successors to the great advocate of historical materialism. But no one seriously advances the view that ideas are unimportant as historical forces.

The big debate is about how they are generated, spread and influence people. In this respect Marxists, precisely because they resisted the over-ambitious claims of sociology, were in the best position to advocate the case for cultural studies. For although sociologists have acknowledged the importance of ideas they have often been more deterministic than the Marxists, tending to treat ideas as determined by society, the position known as sociologism.

We have now to get away from the crude determinisms of the past. The contest between Marxism and sociology was a clash of ideas, not class interests, though politics may have made it appear so, and sociology benefited accordingly. The exchange with cultural studies is equally provocative because for the first time there is a broad-based and systematic approach to the question of just how ideas might help to constitute and change society.

No sociologist now can ignore the importance of the representation of society and social relations through symbols and signs. Anthropologists and philosophers in particular have emphasised this for generations. Early in the century, Thorstein Veblen, a sociologist and economist, pointed out the importance of lavish spending or 'conspicuous consumption' – not for use but to display one's status. Later the idea of the 'status symbol' became commonplace.

But it is largely the new cultural studies which have refocused sociological interest on consumer culture. So is this interest in consumption and fashion as signifying practices just a fashion? No, first of all there are real changes in social relations, in the new variability and flux in people's membership of groups. This clearly brings the focus of attention on to signs of identity. In a crowd you can't tell everyone who you are by speaking to them. There are other ways: the holiday resort T-shirt, the earring, the Rolex watch. Capitalism has geared itself to the consumer and the manufacture of signs is at the centre of advertising. Second, interest in signs may have come into vogue recently but the idea of a science of signs goes back at least to the seventeenth century when it was called semiotics for the first time by the philosopher John Locke.

In the end cultural studies depends on the reality of culture as a life-sphere, where people exercise skills, solve technical problems and develop ideas. It depends on there being occupations in the mass media, museums and galleries, advertising and literary prizes, musicians and theatres. As Max Weber insisted, these have their own directions and logics, which in extreme cases are capable of revolutionising social relations.

There was a time when it was felt that industrial society would eventually generate untold leisure. That optimism changed to gloomy forecasts of mass unemployment. But as Charles Handy pointed out economic and technological change take us beyond employment.[37] Personal, especially cultural, capital increases the chances of moving between employers, and also the possibilities to work on one's own account. But cultural capital, like all aspects of culture, belongs also to constituted groups, and association with them brings its own advantages. It is not accidental that so many doctors come from medical families, or that people seek schools in 'good areas'.

The big political issues of our times concern the extent to which individual educational chances, and hence the opportunity to work, require the state management of collective cultural capital. In studying hard at school or university we make use of collective provision for people to work. The culture of groups is based in facilities and institutions like computers, books, schools and universities which are regularly publicly owned. The politics of education rather than of the workplace has become the arena for social conflict in a society looking beyond employment.

Persons and God

The reason we consider persons in a chapter on social institutions is because the institutional order pivots on them and they are in part the constructs of that order. In other words 'the person' is an institution. In the modern legal order responsibility is imputed to individual persons of sane mind and then a host of behavioural expectations are built into the law, from driving with due care and attention to using only reasonable force in self-defence, quite apart from all those explicit prohibitions of murder, rape, theft.

Further than that there are rights like voting, free movement, free speech, enjoying public facilities which are held to imply civic virtues, responsibilities and duties such as reporting crime, sitting on juries, sending children to school, notifying certain diseases and paying taxes. It is then easy to see that the state, in particular law, not only prohibits certain kinds of behaviour but helps to create the assumptions about what people can expect of each other. But as with all institutions this only crystallises what society creates in the first place, all the way down to a sense of responsibility.

The way society creates persons is a topic in which psychology and sociology join forces. In the public mind Sigmund Freud's theory of sexual repression, guilt and neurosis is probably the most famous.[38]

This has as its premise the interaction of members of the family. But for sociology G.H. Mead was most renowned for his account of the development of the self, the ability to say 'I' about 'me' as a result of interaction with significant others, who then become generalised as the conscience.[39]

Since then the most important contributions have been those which have stressed the political side of the formation of the self. In his account of the development of the Western state, Elias attributed the historical change in patterns of interpersonal behaviour to its acquisition of the monopoly of violence.[40] Foucault argued that sexuality is actually created through what power and discipline forbid and in the refusal to allow the free exploration of bodily pleasure.[41]

It is, then, not only the person which becomes an institution; the body as site of health, fitness, physique, and style is shaped to the requirements of power. The sociology of the body is one of the most keenly researched areas of sociology today, stimulated in large part by Foucault's work. At the same time experiences of the body, in particular the life events of birth, marriage and death in every society have been the focus of institutions which in the West are known as religion. It finds a meaning for life events and at the same time renders some kinds of social relations sacred.

Sociological study no more explains religion away than the sociology of medicine explains away hepatitis. But the sociology of religion does have much to say about incidence; why people join or leave religious groups; about processes of change in the formation of churches, sects and denominations and how they are organised; how religious leaders, priests and prophets exercise control over their believers; and how religion works through society on other spheres of life. Core beliefs have their own logic, again as in any institutional area, borne by social relations but with a degree of autonomy from them and other beliefs. Belief in God is the most free-floating of all beliefs. It can be combined with any or no particular constellation of social relations, and can infuse any institutional sphere.

Decline in belief in God was for a long time considered a key indicator for the onward march of modernisation. Belief in science, parliamentary democracy, urbanisation, industrialisation and everything else in a supposedly relentless process had to involve secularisation too. But probably the highpoint of this thinking was as long ago as 1882 at the height of the controversy on evolution, when the German Friedrich Nietzsche shocked a whole generation by declaring God was dead.[42]

Since the 1970s God has refused to retreat. In the most modern of all nations, the United States, a large majority believe in God and a majority go to church. Moreover, in a time which has been called post-materialist, appeals to abstract values in the fight against disease, hunger and poverty time and again find the strongest support from religious sources. The flashpoint issue of abortion in relation to the world's population is the major point of conflict between religious and secular values, and even here compromise is found possible. The government of Bangladesh enlists the support of its religious leaders, the imams, for population campaigns.

Sociologists have no more need from their own disciplinary standpoint to declare a belief in the existence or non-existence of God than they have in quasars or mad cou disease. It is the way society carries belief which is their concern. On the other hand, where groups diverge on doctrine sociologists may well have to identify the points on which they differ in order to undertake sociological analysis and assess the importance of a particular belief for schism.

The study of dogma, schism and heresy in religion shows how belief can become the focus for group formation for any life-sphere, including politics and science. The fervour and feuds of animal rights activists, Trotskyite groups and the mujahedin may or may not be associated with the idea of God, but they give a good indication of how reality for and of a group can itself turn on faith in the rightness of a cause. Simply because sociologists then have to explore with equal sympathy the positions of 'true' and 'false' believers they are almost bound to come to a view on the logic of their positions. These are conflicts within cultures that they adjudicate from a common-sense standpoint outside them.

In the time when the great schism of the West was between religion and science and sociology declared itself for science it appeared that its task was the discovery of the social sources of error. It is an aspect of the transformation which is called postmodern that science and religion have moved from opposition to collusion in acknowledging their inability to solve great mysteries, of the infinitely large or small, of eternity or the origin of the universe, and also in their acceptance of faith in 'something' as a fact of life.

If in daily life this translates into God the sociologist is the last person to be able to dismiss this as unfounded, given the fact that in contemporary sociological theory the move has been to see society as ungrounded, and ontological security to be based in trust and faith. In the serious study of mystic experience the sociologist is as likely as anyone to end up experiencing the mystic.

It is for this reason that I include God within the life-sphere of Persons rather than State, Work, Environment or Culture. The affinities between the experience of the body as self which reveals the person and the experience of the world as reality revealing God are close enough to suggest why world-wide vastly differing cultural experiences culminate in the idea of God.

Beyond institutionalism

We are finally in a position to return to the question we set at the beginning of the chapter: is there a distinct sphere for society or is it the basis for any life-sphere whatsoever? In one respect all institutions are social. The diffusion of skilled practices over which there is some common control and which are widespread is not possible without their being underpinned by society, complex webs of social relations. In this sense we hardly need to talk of 'social' institutions if they are all social.

At the same time, as we have stressed, the practices themselves and the skills of the practitioners develop or wither through people's active engagement with a world which they either have not made or, in so far as they have, they can never fully control or understand. This is true for the economy, for sea transport or space travel, sport or medicine, education, religion or law.

State, work, environment, culture and the person itself are life-spheres where institutions develop as human beings engage with reality. Social relations are a base for all these engagements. But this book has insisted throughout that society is not equatable with any other sphere and is equally part of reality. In this case there must also be institutions for society just as there are for the state and the other life-spheres.

There are, then, institutions for social relations specifically. The most obvious is the family, found everywhere, past and present but in a vast variety of shapes and forms. It clearly predates the nation-state. In the contemporary world states seek to shape it through marriage law, but increasingly people develop their own parallel understandings of how marriage should work and of partnerships outside marriage. The state has to catch up with social change.

In the case of marriage law it is clear that the state seeks to frame what in any case emerges out of human social relations. Not all social relations do take shape through law. Friendship is a ubiquitous institution which finds no regulation in law in modern societies. On the other hand friends may make a contract with each other which the law will recognise. This recognition of the basis of institutions in the facts of social relations is not confined to first-order social relations. Even nationality, which the nation-state seeks to make the basis of its membership, arises out of a bond between person and nation which in the last resort is the 'effective link', which the law recognises.[43] Equally the right to nationality is for the United Nations a human right, something the law recognises rather than creates. Human rights are a type of relation we have to human beings in general; third-order social relations in other words.

The stabilisation of social relations through institutions is a universal feature of society. But a doctrine which asserts that the purpose of institutions is to stabilise society mistakes means for ends. The order that arises out of institutionalised practices secures an active collective engagement with the world.

Institutionalist theories which emphasise the stabilisation functions of rules for society plainly are in the interests of those who control institutions. But then institutional stability is useful for anyone who wants to get on with their job. To this extent the new institutionalism in economics is an advance because it stresses the enabling functions of institutions.

At the same time unless we recognise that getting on with the job always means exploring beyond the standard and routine, in other words activity in the world not just practice, then we are unprepared to face the ever-renewed challenge to institutions which honest human endeavour represents. The economist Oliver Williamson has shown how differing institutional arrangements have important consequences for the working of organisations.[44] Those arrangements are the adaptive repertoire which society has available as the balance between individual and collective activity changes.

However, there is more than economic benefit at stake with human activity. The institutions which frame the social relations of work are, as Marx asserted, vulnerable to the productive forces they release, but there is no reason to think that they will be reshaped simply with economic ends in view. Indeed there is every reason to think that culture and the environment, the spheres where today social relations are least fettered by the state, will become increasingly powerful forces in shaping the institutions of the next century.

Finally the guardians of institutions have to realise that those divisions between sectors of activity which they then call institutions like education, medicine, sport, business, technology, science, and so on are purely the current outcomes of human adaptation to a world and environment we have in part made. Their boundaries are always shifting and areas come and go. For instance, information technology is a new area, crossing others and involving widespread institutional change. The changes which are the most painful are not the acceptance of new machines nor the acquisition of new skills. It is the recrafting of social relations, and this is where we need to draw not only on our ideals but also on our knowledge of how far it is possible to realise them. We need the science of institutions as well as ideals for them and science in them.

Chapter 5

Society in
the Future

Open futures

The ignorance society

Practical people in the Modern Age were optimists
because they felt they could direct the world to their
desired goals. In the American Dream a whole country
adhered to this faith in themselves and the future. As
an acute German immigrant observed about Americans
'Neither race nor tradition, nor yet the actual past bind
him to his countryman, but rather the future which
together they are building.'[1]

In Europe this was a confidence which was also
shared by the socialists before Marx. When Robert
Owen (1771–1858), one of the founders of socialism,
wrote an account of his own life in the mid-nineteenth
century he felt, like so many others, that there were
no limits to growth. For him development was always
sustainable. Men had the means to create harmony
with nature 'and to their increase there can be no
assignable limits ... The means for universal human
happiness are inexhaustible.'[2]

European intellectuals after Marx were less sanguine, and his gloom about human alienation and intensification of class struggle may have been extreme but was not untypical. On the right of the political spectrum there was similar pessimism about loss of community and mass irrationality. Max Weber viewed the rationalisation of the world as a process in which we know less and less about the conditions of our everyday lives: 'The savage knows incomparably more about his tools.'[3]

We live in what some have called a 'Knowledge Society',[4] but this does not eliminate ignorance.[5] Put another way, it just means our ignorance sets in later. We often talk of expanding the frontiers of knowledge; but, using this territorial metaphor, the other side of the boundary is ignorance. So, as knowledge expands, the knowledge/ignorance border gets longer all the time.

Every sphere of knowledge provides examples of this. We discover 'black holes' in space, new knowledge; we don't know how they come into being, new ignorance: we find vaccines for diseases, new knowledge; we don't know how new viruses arise which overcome the vaccines, new ignorance: we invent computers, new opportunities; we create millennium bugs, new threat.

In this new Ignorance Society we are surrounded by hazards which are the consequences of our earlier blind faith in applied science. Soil exhaustion, pollution, extinction of species, global warming are side effects of our endeavours which Ulrich Beck argues mean we are divided by our exposure to risk more than by inequalities of wealth.[6]

It is not only in our ability to control nature for human ends that we have lost confidence. Sociologists from Robert Merton onwards have also stressed the unanticipated consequences of our attempts to organise society.[7] Humankind doesn't work together as a single agent, and there is no way we can predict the outcomes of all its activities when taken together. Even if it did work to a single co-ordinated plan we would have to concede a place to the unknown workings of the non-human world.

The profundity of our ignorance, not just mine and yours but also of every scientist, no matter how eminent, is one of the basic conditions of human existence and hence of society and sociology itself. In our time we have lost the presumptuous faith of modernity that it could control the world. The known frontiers of society provide it with very limited space in the world as a whole.

Society is less than the human species, which is less than life and creation. Society has to compete for our attention with life-spheres it does not control like economy, religion, culture, and it can't even control people. But in turn it resists control and requires as much knowledge as any other sphere on the part of those who claim concern for it.

The control freaks

We have sufficient distance from the core ideas of old modernity to be able to dismiss as naive the idea of uncheckable human progress. But this was not the only idea at the heart of modernity. Another was the general belief that history was about the development of society. In the old Modern Age for so many the future of society was the same thing as *the* future. We can see that especially with the old socialists. Planning for the future meant above all the reorganisation of society, changing relations between classes, or abolishing them altogether, creating ideal communities, securing perfect equality between the sexes, or a world-wide community of nations.

Idealism time and again meant imagining a new society. But that is only one aspect of our future. We can, and should, if we want to lead full lives, also direct our concerns elsewhere. There are other ideals like love, wisdom, or creativity. Although they can never be realised except in and through society, they may be quite neutral in respect of different types of social relations, a view which priests, artists or scientists have often expressed.

The problem for those who have often been called social engineers is that a lot else happens besides, in addition to, or in spite of their blueprints for future society. History, past, present and future, is much more than the story of changes in the organisation of society. Population growth, new communication media, automation, nuclear power, biological engineering, new age religions and consumerism involve qualitative changes in ways of living which are often independent of particular types of society. But equally they can affect social relations as much as being a product of them. So many of these features contribute to the insecurity and uncertainty of the future, precisely because they appear to change the assumptions on which society has rested in the past.

What the twentieth century found was that technical functions and cultural patterns cross boundaries and invade all kinds of societies irrespective of their constitution. The trade union, the department store, the victim support group all use information technology. Couples in socialist and liberal societies each adopt contraceptive methods. Christians and Muslims each buy ready-made meals. Air transport spans the world.

Sometimes these changes are simply put together and called 'social change'. But a moment's thought should be sufficient for recognising that when we talk in terms of changes to people's lives we mean much more than changes to society, or how our social relations are organised. These are changes to the way we experience the world, to the 'life-world' and its spheres, of which society is just one aspect.

Because as individuals what we do extends far further than simply engaging in social relations, and because collectively our efforts result in much more than maintaining or changing society, our world is far more extensive and open-ended than anything that can be imagined in a blueprint for a new society.

The blueprint makers have often in effect recognised this by trying to control everything. The more intolerant and dogmatic of the sociologists, such as Auguste Comte, who claimed he was on the way to completing knowledge, along with socialists of the totalitarian kind, saw that ideas and products are capable of unleashing forces which at best bypass, at worst tear apart, any particular social ordering. Time and again the would-be society makers have tried to contain ideas but always in the end in vain. Equally they have relied on taming the natural world and putting it exclusively to human uses. But it always kicks back at them.

These dreamers seek to subordinate history, the story of the human species in the world, to society. In fact they see history as the story of society, culminating and ending in its perfection. We can now see that this project is doomed to failure. The future is open even when society is closed.

Accounting for change

Surviving the present

Human interest in society is very practical and not a matter of mere curiosity. Because society is the bearer of all human activities we need to know where we stand in relation to it in order to get on with our lives. But the message of this book is that society is both a variegated landscape and a fluid medium, repeatedly shaken up by the winds of change. Most of that change results from the unplanned effects of human action in a world we have not made, where society is a core element.

Trying to get hold of this elusive core without distorting it is demanding and calls for patient observation and clearly directed effort. At the same time the kind of theory we need varies according to the direction of our interest. Change in first-order social relations, in families, is very different from change in the third order, in human rights. At the same time they are not sealed off from each other and it is fundamental to understand their linkages. Thus the aggregate of changes in families has quantifiable consequences for world population growth. Indeed there is a chain which links having children with the future of society.

World population and the family provide the best example of the successful application of linked theories which operate both for the globe and in personal lives. For several decades social scientists have collaborated with the United Nations, national and voluntary agencies to develop a policy which could curb world population growth. Decades of research have shown how population changed in the West in the period of demographic transition in the late nineteenth century when mortality was low and fertility high, from a state when both were high to the point where both stabilised at a low level. Historians, social scientists and demographers have been able to identify the cluster of factors which were most important in bringing birth rates down, including the employment and equality of women and the high cost of children.

But the demographic transition was still a process which took decades and the West became concerned that population in the rest of the world would grow too fast for available world resources.

In consequence, from the 1970s programmes to restrict population growth were initiated in a co-ordinated world campaign. After a false start when it was assumed education and contraception would be sufficient, these policies have centred on promoting women's rights, health and economic independence, and as a result world population growth has slowed faster than could otherwise have been expected and is likely to stabilise at perhaps double the present size of near six billion in the mid-twenty-first century. This is not a fast enough rate of decline from many points of view, including our concern for the environment, but at least we do not now envisage uncontrolled growth into the indefinite future.

Not every country, nor every agency, has co-operated. China went its own way with its one-child policy, continuing a tradition both of central control and population planning. The Catholic Church in Rome has resisted every attempt to restrict family size except through sexual abstinence. Controversy has remained intense throughout the period. But overall the fact is that a global policy for people's lives world-wide has been implemented with identifiable effects.

It tells us a lot about theory in a changing world. For a start we need both a telescopic sight and wide-angle lens for past and future, allied with microscopic focus on individual behaviour within primary, secondary and tertiary social relations and in all the life-spheres. Working out what we should do in the present, both for public policy and private purposes, therefore needs both history and the social sciences.

This illustrates how important time perspectives are for understanding society. We can distinguish three main ones. We can first view human society in terms of problems of the human condition which recur in all times and places. We have always had to cope with problems of birth and death, relations between men, women and children, the natural environment, nutrition, illness, work, education, conflict, deviant behaviour. The problems are universal, they are expressed differently in different times and places and answers vary in innumerable ways, but they always involve society, not just individual people. Very often the universality of the problems and the limited range of solutions which seems to exist to them has encouraged sociologists to write of them as the 'social system'.

Second, we can observe that particular social arrangements have extraordinarily varying lifespans. The specific answers to the universal problems vary both over time and place and much of sociology is concerned to record and explain these passing phenomena. For 2,000 years the Chinese thought that social order depended on the Emperor – until 1911. In the West it was once thought that the Welfare State was here to stay indefinitely and this has now been challenged fundamentally – in part because societies like the Chinese do not have it. These differing durations in all their cultural variety encourage the opposite kind of writing to that of stress on system. Rather these become ephemeral phenomena.

Third, we can identify cumulative social changes with roots far back in the past which appear to allow humankind no way back. The growth of science and technology and human dependence on them, world population, the enclosure of land, the size and scale of human organisation appear to have produced irreversible effects on the environment and to have changed permanently the basis on which to provide answers to the universal problems. Even if we try to return to a simple way of life, close to nature, the rest of society roars overhead and alongside. This irreversibility has led many to reflect on development, because development is a form of growth which cannot be reversed, although it can be arrested or terminated.

These are three basic problem settings in sociological accounts, each as important as the other and each vital for understanding society. But overemphasis on one of them to the neglect of the other two will lead to a distorted view of society. The danger words to look out for in this respect are 'system', 'phenomena' and 'development'. No general theory of society should treat these concepts as more than aids to understanding. Society is not a system because it can be transformed; the variety of social phenomena does not mean that anything we imagine is possible; the fact of development does not sweep all before it.

In some ways the most fraught term of all which seeks to bring history and science together for the study of society is 'evolution'. The success of Darwin's work in the nineteenth century in solving many of the puzzles of the origins of biological species proved that science could and needed to penetrate the distant past. It also suggested parallels with Spencer's thinking in sociology which likened the growing complexity of society to the emergence of more complex biological organisms.

With the popular reception of the phrases 'survival of the fittest' and 'struggle for existence', promoted by what became known as Social Darwinism,[8] the scene was set for attempts to relate the survival of society to the breeding of people of superior physique. What began as academic inquiry and liberal concern for public health, took form as the eugenics movement and ended up in the 1930s as Nazi racism. This fateful historical sequence has tarnished many ideas by association, and among them evolution.

In fact the idea of evolution can be applied across the sciences without any reference to biological species or health. It simply refers to the ongoing outcome of competition between units of any kind in an environment where there are limited resources necessary for their reproduction. In this sense, for instance, we can talk of the evolution of industrial organisation without any reference to the health of the workers, and certainly not to their genes!

Indeed, so-called 'natural selection' does not privilege genes above any other kind of entity in determining the outcome of a sequence of events. Human collectivities can drastically reduce the gene pools of plants and animals and often eliminate them altogether. If scientists modify human biological inheritance it demonstrates that they and not genetics are more important for the evolution of society. Darwin himself declared that reasoning and religion were more important for the 'highest part of man's nature' than the struggle for existence.[9]

Evolution is a crucial concept for sociology, not because it points to any necessary direction in history, nor because it shows that there is one mechanism for change, but quite the opposite. It draws attention to the ever-changing requirements for survival in environments which change. These requirements will vary in accord with the size and complexity of the units which compete. This makes it impossible to say that any one practice in society always has less survival value than another. It depends on the unit in which it is lodged in the conditions which prevail.

Sibling incest was institutionalised among the ancient Egyptians whose civilisation lasted millennia. Gassing of Jews, gypsies, homosexuals and the mentally ill was institutionalised by the Nazis. The Third Reich was meant to last a thousand years and just reached a decade. It collapsed as a result of concerted organisation by other Western countries, not, sadly, from their moral concern. Neither their survival value within those societies nor revulsion was sufficient to determine the fates of the practices.

Nor do the size and complexity of society guarantee survival. This was the theory in the early years of sociology favoured by Spencer and Durkheim. As population grew and intensity of interaction increased so society would become more complex, replacing simpler types of social organisation. They saw Western societies as the culmination of an overall development.

The most important refutation of this thesis came from the work of Arnold Toynbee whose study of world civilisations showed that increases of size and complexity hitherto have never been sufficient to ward off eventual collapse.[10] He centred his account on the success or failure of civilisations to respond to challenges. This has variously been called positivistic or mystical. It may be both at once. It didn't solve the problem of why, after successful responses, eventually there was failure. But then neither have biologists solved the problem of why organisms grow.

Grand narrative

The appreciation of the importance of the past for understanding the present predates professional sociology. Indeed it predates disciplines in the modern sense altogether. When Ferguson wrote his enormously influential history of civil society in 1767 he felt it necessary to answer the question of where human society in an original state of nature could be found. His answer was 'it is here', by which he meant that some features of human society were ever present, while others were genuinely new. Distinctively modern were things like property, pacification and citizenship.[11] 'Civil' for him meant both civilian and being civilised in war and could not be attributed to the ancients. But this then was a quality which could equally be lost. It was only in the nineteenth century that Comte, Spencer, Marx and Darwin tried to turn these fragile civil accomplishments, a narrative of progress, into the iron laws of history.

The subordination of history to the idea of relentless progress is what the French philosopher Jean-François Lyotard declared in 1979 to be at an end.[12] He was asked by the Canadian government to produce a report on the contemporary state of knowledge and argued that it was no longer possible to view the past and to justify present action in terms of ever-advancing human freedom or the growth of mind. Instead he found growth of technology, or rather a myriad of technical devices, without any unifying principles. There was no sense of plot or direction. He called this the 'postmodern condition'.

Lyotard wasn't the first to use the idea of the postmodern. His most prominent predecessors were Toynbee and the sociologist C. Wright Mills.[13] But he was the most effective in developing the idea that somehow the modern has been displaced by the postmodern – *whatever that might be*. For once the idea of direction and plot are ruled out it appears doubtful that we can make sense of the time in which we live and say it is this or that period. If we are no longer modern, we appear to have no guidance as to what we are.

The idea of the grand narrative is very important for sociologists because it brings out into the open features of their work which they have often taken for granted. Comte promoted sociology as a separate scientific discipline by claiming it was the culmination of human progress. This became an embarrassment to his successors, but ever since there has been a deep assumption that somehow sociology represents a modern approach and is part of an overall project to make the world a better place.

Most would think that 170 years is enough of a chance to show whether sociology can work. But how many would say that the world is better as a result, or even at all? I might seek to defend my colleagues and myself and say there hasn't been enough sociology. That would, however, be dishonest if I didn't also admit that sociologists worked for the Nazis and that the architect of South Africa's apartheid system was Verwoerd, who was also a sociologist. So sociology's participation in this great project, for which the grand narrative of advancing freedom and knowledge tells the story, is dubious to say the least.

We have a choice. We can delete sociology's part in the grand narrative and treat it as a false start. Many would like to do this, especially if they think that technology and business guarantee endless progress. Alternatively we take another look at grand narrative. It is not simply a nineteenth-century creation, nor does it depend on the idea of inevitable laws of history. The earliest substantial example is 2,500 years old. This is how the Greek-speaking Herodotus introduced his great account of the wars between the Greeks and the Persians:

> In this book, the result of my inquiries into history, I hope to do two things: to preserve the memory of the past by putting on record the astonishing achievements both of our own and of the Asiatic peoples; secondly, and more particularly, to show how the two races came into conflict.[14]

Now Herodotus was writing of his own time as 'history' and that Greek word meant simply inquiry. In fact Herodotus' method is now more recognisable to us as sociology, for it involved travelling, recording the customs of different countries, interviewing participants in big events, collecting popular stories and reading documents. But he makes it something more than a mass of materials because he shapes them into an overall story. And the way he does that hasn't changed much since. The main actors in the drama are peoples, us and the others; they achieve great things and come into conflict. Herodotus differs from the modern chauvinist in his respect both for the other side and for the facts. The professional sociologist differs from him in questioning the construction of the story: can we assume that the grand narrative is one of 'peoples' with proper names like Asiatics and Greeks?

Not everyone in the nineteenth century believed in the laws of history. The Herodotean narrative was continued by the outstanding foreign observer of America, Alexis de Tocqueville. He concluded his great study of democracy with a lightning account of its development from the Middle Ages when there were innumerable divisions between peoples and looked forward to the time when America would be one nation of 150 million people, rivalled only by Russia.

> There are now two great nations in the world, which starting from different points seem to be advancing toward the same goal; the Russians and the Anglo Americans ... One has freedom as the principal means of action; the other has servitude. Their point of departure is different and their paths diverse; nevertheless, each seems called by some secret design of Providence one day to hold in its hands the destinies of half the world.[15]

De Tocqueville's prophecy of 1848 came true for a time in the Cold War between 1945 and 1989. Unlike his contemporary, Marx, he was content to leave the question of the future to a 'secret design'. He could see trends but no underlying plot. This is grand narrative without a direction, but it establishes our place in the moving order of time.

Hundreds of books continue to take the grand narrative forward. A recent one declares that 'human history is the history of civilizations' and these turn out to be Egyptian, Classical, Christian, Islamic, Sinic and others. The author, Samuel Huntington, quotes Herodotus as saying they are marked off one from another by blood, language, religion, way of life.[16] Like de Tocqueville he sees the narrative tending to the possibility of a global war between 'the biggest player in the history of man' China and the United States, core state of the West.[17]

Huntington was director of security planning for President Carter's America. His grand narrative then draws on the experience of real world politics. This is what we have to bear in mind, the story of the achievements of peoples and the clash of civilisations is not just a story, it provides the plot for those who want to find a direction in world events. Politics and the media recruit people to become extras in the great drama of their own times, encouraging them to speak lines like 'better dead than red'. The grand narrative becomes a real part of public discourse.

Indeed what this illustrates is that we cannot make sense of the time in which we live, even in our personal lives, without a grand narrative. The issue is: what kind of narrative? The answer has to be one which reflects our understanding of the new ignorance; that is, the limits of our knowledge and the unpredictability of evolution.

We no longer have the unbounded optimism of the nineteenth century, even if we have found it possible to restrain the growth of the world's population. There has been a dramatic transformation of the world in the last 50 years so that it is more one place than ever before. We may indeed be persuaded that new global interdependence outweighs the clash of civilisations. We are in the Global Age in which we have to understand world society as a reality, not a dream.[18] But the nature of that society is open for inquiry and for our determined collective wills.

The future of capitalism

Capitalist society

The best way in the late 1990s to clarify what society will be like in an open future is to tackle the issue of capitalism. That hasn't always been the case, but very often these days society's future is treated as identical with the future of capitalism, sometimes even as capitalist society without end.

This ought to make us wary. In human history this idea is relatively new. Before the latter part of the nineteenth century it never occurred to anyone that there was such a thing as 'capitalism' or that it could mark a distinctive type of society. So the novelty of the idea should make us sit up. At the same time we need to recognise that all kinds of 'new' society have withered away, even as society in general has continued. On past experience we might then expect that society will outlive capitalism, or, at least, that a time will come when we think of capitalist society as belonging to the past, which is not quite the same thing.

This last point may be subtle, but it is equally vital. A society dominated by a particular set of qualities may pass away, even though those qualities may persist in a less prominent fashion. For example, 'feudal society', one in which loyalties and obligations to the holder of a status underpin political institutions over generations, has undeniably ended in the West. But while it lost its dominance by the eighteenth century and may have effectively ceased to exist by the beginning of the twentieth century, feudal elements live on continuously to the present (think of the British Royal Household). We also frequently find reinventions of feudal conditions even within capitalism. One writer has written of some corporations in the United States creating 'modern manors' even as they promote 'welfare capitalism'. It suggest that in this case feudalism and capitalism can actually support each other.[19]

So we have to be careful to distinguish different continuities. Capitalism could live on, society in general will surely continue, but capitalist society might pass away, and all at the same time. The continuity of capitalism, the future of society and the future of capitalist society are each rather different issues. If initially we explore how capital first became related to the idea of capitalism, and then again how this was linked to society to become 'capitalist society', we are already on our way to exploring the conditions for the end of capitalist society! This might seem to be the stuff of revolutionary dreams, but the logic fits the known historical facts, that types of society pass away even without the thought or practice of revolution.

With Marx you start with money but you get back through industry to society. And this organisation of society is dependent on the development of human productive powers, a general theory of history that he and his colleague Engels called 'the materialist conception of history'. Marx only occasionally mentioned 'capitalism' and it was only after his death that this became a common expression. Capitalists for him were not the agents of capitalism, they were the owners of capital. (Just as artists make art and are not the agents of 'artism'!)

The 'ism' of 'capitalism' makes it an abstract idea, something which can inspire people, and Marx and Engels advanced historical materialism as an alternative to the view that history was the product of ideas. Capital is the outcome of the practical strivings of workers in their relations with capitalists, an ongoing process of social relations.

Now, as we saw in Chapter 1, by the end of the twentieth century it has become commonplace to refer to any set of requirements for the increase of humanity's future well-being as 'capital'. If Marx took the idea of capital through a sequence of society, money, industry and back to society, today the sequence is society, money, industry, science, arts, skills, society, at least.

So we now talk of capitalist society and it takes on a much more extensive and at the same time different meaning from the bourgeois society of Marx's time. It means a society dominated by capitalism, rather than by a class of capitalists. For as capital has come to absorb this great range of human and cultural factors, at the same time, and related to it, an ever-growing proportion of the population owns some capital and engages in capitalist activity. Capitalism relies on ordinary people saving and borrowing money, gaining qualifications, buying houses as well as consuming products which go far beyond daily subsistence.

There is still a capitalist class, with untold wealth, capable of supporting a lifestyle far removed from the overwhelming majority of people who glimpse it in the pages of 'society' magazines rather than confront it in their daily labours. But the owners of big capital can also choose to lose themselves in the crowd and owners of tiny assets can conduct their lives on capitalist principles. As capital has expanded so the boundaries between classes have both multiplied and blurred. It's the capitalist system which permeates society, not the employers' dictates.

The limits of capitalism

It may be commonplace but we cannot ignore feelings of discomfort with the idea that almost anything can be, or become, capital. For it inscribes the whole of humanity's mission on the accountant's balance sheet. We sense, as part of our collective memory, that capital meant originally money, and we know that calling anything 'capital' means attributing a money value to it. It is still a way of talking which challenges us to ask how it might be otherwise. Surely money is not the only measure of worth.

In particular it prompts us to seek to recover times past when the world was not capitalist. Ever since Marx the history of capitalism has therefore been of prime interest for anyone exploring alternative possibilities for society. If we take a long enough historical view we can appreciate the special conditions which provided for the development of capitalism. We can now see more clearly how from the sixteenth century onwards the Modern Age in Western Europe and

America involved the subordination of every aspect of human activity to drives to explore and expand human control of nature and society. So much so that the organisation of society was dominated by what has been called 'the Modern Project'.

The world became a project and this was crystallised in the modern state and the modern capitalist firm. The capitalism of today is the outcome of that project, but so also is mass democracy, universal education, global communications and the United Nations. All this is bigger than just 'capitalism' and many would put it under a broader umbrella with the term 'modernisation'.

Within this broad notion of modernisation we can see that capitalism is not everything. For example it is not democracy, which may or may not be linked to it, and the nature of the linkage may be very variable. We can find places where capitalism intrudes on democracy; for instance in long-standing attempts to limit democracy to those who own property. This is putting a non-democratic principle in place, voting according to wealth, which makes 'shareholder democracy' almost self-contradictory. Yet should the owner of one share have the same rights as the owner of a million?

On the other hand politics can dictate the place of capitalism, as when the Chinese Communist Party introduces capitalism to serve its own purposes and when fascist states set capitalism to work for the aggressive nationalism which led to the Second World War. These inherent limits to capitalism are not simply political. If we think of all the things which are called capital today they go far beyond money and machinery. They extend to land, roads, vehicles, education, training, patents, brands and images; social, cultural and human resource capital as well as financial and industrial capital. Nothing which cannot be put to the creation of future wealth by a person or group is in principle ignored. It's a very big bundle indeed.

But then it is so big that we have to wonder whether it is properly labelled as 'capital'. For instance, social capital has been defined as 'trust, norms and networks that can improve the efficiency of society'.[20] But equally they may not improve 'efficiency', just as not all learning is cultural capital. Transcendental meditation may help stressed business leaders to do a better job, but it also might encourage them to get out of the rat race. After all if we consider together imagination, resources, skills, vision and our relations to selves and nature we might equally label the parcel 'religion'. Life and its meaning are both wholly implicated in 'capital' and 'religion' if they are understood to extend so far.

Now we begin to realise that while both capital and religion may each seek to embrace everything, nothing is exclusively theirs unless human beings treat it so. The glories of the Sistine Chapel in Rome could be dismantled and become art commodities worth millions of dollars. Where they rest they are literally priceless, sacred icons of a world religion.

Not that the boundaries between capital and religion are always so clear. The tourist souvenir from a visit to the Chapel may have a purchase value far beyond the materials and labour expended on it. Religion is then exploited as a resource, even by those engaged in it. But it is a relation full of tension. Jesus Christ did not throw the moneylenders out of the temple simply in a fit of pique.

This may help to explain why the relation of religion and capitalism was so important for Max Weber. He saw how they competed to make sense of and determine the direction of human activities. But he also saw them conspiring together in the modern period to subordinate society to objectives which were independent of human will.

The examples of the relations of religion and capitalism, or of politics and capitalism, are only instances of the general point that human activities have an extended repertoire of concerns and that no particular agenda can permanently dominate or exclude the others. Their relations are ever-changing and they each help to set the limits of the others.

The reason key features of the human condition have become known as capital rather than religion in the last two hundred years is because of a fundamental transformation of the ordering of human social relations in the Western world. Long-standing relations between feudal lord and tenants became disposable junk when peasants were turned off land in favour of the sheep. The industrial and agricultural revolutions of the Modern Age treated social relations as technical means to ends, as the basis for future wealth.

The fruit of this was always a product which could promote the further development of the project: capital, in the broadest sense the resources on which the future is based. Deep down this is impersonal. The discourse of 'human resources', 'human capital' converts personal skills and capacities into means to ends, rather than the realisation of humanity. In this sense modern social relations and the identities which went with them were potentially always candidates for asset/liability or profit/loss accounting.

For many sociologists this has marked off modern societies from all that went before, which in the broadest sense are therefore to be called 'traditional'. In these premodern societies human purposes did not dictate the nature of society. Rather purposes emerged in a determinate frame of social relations. As people pursued their purposes they effectively reproduced the old society. On this account the question of changing society, let alone creating an ideal society, simply did not arise.

This view of premodern societies being 'traditional' exaggerates their stability and continuity. In the ancient European world both Greeks and Romans consciously experimented with the form of society and religion was always capable of challenging established patterns of life. There were ways for humanity to challenge the form of society before the Modern Age.

Even for Marx it was human agency which produced the inhumanity and alienation of capitalist society. Capitalists, not an abstract modernity, confronted the working class. But by the time of Weber the forces of modernity have become capitalism as a system and a spirit, and the specific character of modern society is its progressive dehumanisation. If capital and the purposes of impersonal agencies dominate the world then social relations can no longer embody distinctively human needs.

Marx, by challenging a class-divided society, put universal humanity on the intellectual agenda. He made the organisation of society not just a technical matter of best arrangements for present purposes, but the very realisation of what it was to be human, the stimulus for world-wide socialism. Paradoxically it produced the total subordination of society in state socialism. At the same time it prompted the defensive reactions of state and capitalist organisation.

Ever since, sociology has worked with the problem-setting which prompted Marx's concerns and which gave the leaders of

Western nation-states so much worry. They were haunted by an ever-present danger of the collapse of society and its future became the main theme of any account of the present. But bringing society back into the frame of our considerations is manifestly not sufficient either to explain history or to control the future. Nor does it guarantee the values of humanity.

The reality of society impresses us both by its vulnerability to outside forces and by our inability to control it for human ends. There are many aspects to society's autonomy. There are unanticipated consequences of human activities for social relations; there is resistance to efforts to control from within a society; there are countervailing forces from other societies; there are impacts of environmental factors on society, disease, famine, flood.

We can therefore see why society is not the safest form of investment for the capitalist. As a resource it is unpredictable and unreliable and resists being subordinated to the idea of capital. Social relations, in comparison with other types of capital, like finance, machines, designs, land, may be more durable but they can switch from being assets to being liabilities overnight. At the same time there is no clear direction in their history.

In the contemporary world it is dangerous to place excessive reliance on either personal relations or on larger social entities if you want to amass capital. Partners and firms can free themselves of you as easily as you can decide to free yourselves from them. Emotional attachments are more readily given to symbolic points of stability like football teams since they will not respond by rejecting you. Alternatively the national tie provides a security because so many will just accept it as a fact and it is portable from place to place. But the tension between nation and capital is never ending.

Scenarios

Grand narrative seeks to grasp the future of humankind and humanity. It's that big picture which professionals who work within the different life-spheres, the servants of the institutions and the academic disciplines, find it difficult to see in the round. This is why the idea of the postmodern travelled from Toynbee's bird's-eye view of a new period of history to Lyotard's rejection of the possibility of seeing any periods at all.

But when the specialists come together they still seek to find an account of the world which they can share. If the specialism is highly segregated in training and outlook then this sometimes simply becomes the world from their special viewpoint. A prime example of this is in medicine, so influential that it has almost made the word 'specialist' synonymous with the doctor with a specialism. The view of the world from a medical point of view can make every aspect of life from childbirth to death a medical problem, something Ivan Illich dubbed the 'medicalization of life'.[21]

It is when specialists from many disciplines seek to work together that these special professional viewpoints have to find some common ground. This happens in government, in serving the state, and political leaders have a common interest in producing a grand narrative of the world. In the last ten years they have worked hard to produce the discourse of globalisation, of the world as one place, which has become stock in trade for journalists and academics as well as politicians. It has had particular appeal for business too.

The business world is a sector of life where a variety of professionals come together. But it also has a considerable interest in the whole picture and the future. Investment decisions depend on that for a start. We may recall capital as a store of value *for the future*. It therefore depends on a view of where the world is going. Thus it is now generally held that there is strong evidence for the onset of global warming. A global insurance company like Munich Re, which insures the insurance companies of the world, takes account of this in setting its rates. But the environment is only one part of the world picture.

The problem is weighting the different contributions. Very different outcomes are possible, depending on how much importance we accord to the impact of political instability as compared with new energy sources, population growth or technological innovation. This uncertainty has given rise to a new kind of history of the future, the scenario, a plausible projection of the future, based on certain assumptions, usually pitted against equally plausible alternatives, pioneered by Herman Kahn and the Rand Corporation, and extensively used by transnational corporations like Shell.

In scenarios society does not usually appear as a distinct consideration. However, the past record of sociologists for speculative projections into the future is rather good. Daniel Bell was at the forefront of predicting trends in post-industrial society before business took it seriously.[22] Alvin Toffler, who has become a guru in the business and political world, has similarly been very successful with anticipating the future flexible society.[23]

As both active politician and sociologist Senator Daniel P. Moynihan is notable for having been almost alone in predicting the collapse of the Soviet Union.[24] He was able to give due importance to the problem of ethnicity. The West mobilised a multicultural, international society in a way the Soviets were unable to do even within their own borders. In this respect the Second World War was decisive for the West in that it had to confront and defeat the racism in its own midst. Victory over fascism was the prerequisite for victory over communism.

There are good reasons why sociology should be an effective disciplinary foundation for scenario production, but rather few have recognised them. The reason is that changes in society are basically too slow-moving to grab daily headlines. They are also deep-seated and below the surface, have ramifying effects throughout institutions and, once entrenched, difficult to shift. Configurations of social relations viewed globally do not change overnight. The Soviet Union was a relatively fragile set of arrangements for governance straddling historic ethnicities which were far more enduring. Those represented a permanent source of strain which, with a small increment of pressure, led to collapse.

Sociologically grounded scenarios have to take a lot into account: capital ownership, globalisation, governance, new technology, population trends – and we have to see these in relation to the universal problems and human aspirations. Sociologists looking to the future on a global scale are bound to see capital in terms of social relations. We can see the rise of a global class which manages the global systems of state and capital. But it is unlikely to confront the rest of society given that it is not challenged in the way old national ruling classes were. And its membership will be quite fluid.

Indeed, in sociological terms globalisation may well have paradoxical consequences. If it is no longer the politics of nation-states which produce the great solidarities, and if capital itself becomes more fluid across frontiers, we may expect other older non-spatial types of bonding, as well as ethnicity, to become more prominent. We can look to the growing importance of dynasties, based on kin, natural and adopted children, to become the locus of capital transmission. We may expect the great business networks to depend on cronies, halfway between friends and business partners, collaborative arrangements for mutual exchange rather than common advantage.

From this viewpoint the great transnational corporations may have shorter and shorter lives, becoming much more like special ventures and projects, built out of coalitions of cronies in the global financial system, knowledge-based groups and dynasties. This sounds dark and forbidding. I could have said families and friends, motherhood and apple pie. But that would not capture the specific ways time and space, generation and wealth are built into social relations with dynasties and cronies.

Nor is this as pessimistic as it might be. We could merge both dynasties and cronies into Mafia and Triads and anticipate the wholesale privatisation of law and order, the triumph of force and fraud. But there are big countervailing forces to any doom scenario. The first is democracy, not as the mass democracy of nation-states, with majorities asserting their will over oppressed minorities, but a democracy emerging out of the transnational relations of a multiplicity of campaigning groups. Sometimes called 'globalisation from below', or 'cosmopolitan democracy', the idea of global citizenship will capture the imagination of more and more people world-wide.[25] The work of movements like Amnesty and Friends of the Earth relies on individual commitments to humanity on a worldwide basis.

The other force is the knowledge interests of the global class which know no boundaries. The universality of knowledge has always broken national frameworks even when funding has been national. But now capitalistic interests actively support world-wide research and education. The educational funding in Eastern Europe provided by billionaire global financier George Soros is one example. The institutionalisation of the pursuit of knowledge is world-wide and makes the academy the central human collectivity in the reproduction of old and production of new values, more important than parliaments or churches.

But this kind of scenario clearly comes from the academy, probably overestimating its own influence and ability to see into the future. After all, tomorrow the asteroid might hit us. On the other hand sociologists do have an interest in getting others to take account of their concern for society in the present.

Towards a human society

Specialisation and reductionism

At the heart of sociology there has to be, and usually has been, a recognition that some problems for society never go away, that social arrangements are inherently transitory and that on some changes there is no going back. These are pivotal features of human society and actually make it different in nature from other subjects of study. So human society is not like insect society, rock formation, biological organism, engine, computer or game of chess. It has its own distinctive characteristics and sociologists have both the knowledge and the responsibility for pointing this out.

Recognition of the importance of preserving unique parts of creation is widespread now in natural sciences, art and literature. We are anxious to preserve the gene pool of plants and animal species, to retain unique habitats, to prevent the destruction of archaeological sites, to save languages. Human society is equally very special and deserves appropriate care and attention. Sociologists are also in the preservation business.

One of the main threats to unique creations is using them for human purposes which actually destroy their nature: treating a species as mere food, a Roman camp as a tourist site, or a language as a mere means of transmitting information. In each case something is reduced to something else.

This kind of reduction happens to society too. Human relations are treated as adjuncts to business, as part of a national plan, or as selective breeding devices. Sociology, like any other discipline looking after its cherished subject, is always on the alert for this kind of reductionism. We can't permit society to be treated as anything different from what it is. So this also means putting up warning signs to other disciplines not to colonise what is not in their care.

This relationship between subjects is often trivialised and treated as just a matter of professional or trade rivalry, like chemists not being allowed to set up as doctors. But it is a question of specialism. However inadequate your own doctor may be, it is very dangerous if you are ill to rely on the pharmacy for cure. Health cannot be reduced to taking the right drugs and the medical profession has lost esteem to the extent that it gives that impression.

Similarly, caring for society is not just a matter of getting the economy right, devising corporate plans, finding the right land-use pattern, reforming the law, avoiding genetic defects. Of course success in these fields is important and we depend on specialists to deliver it. But they don't in themselves provide for the good society. Indeed, far from the specialists making it unnecessary to devote special attention to society, they need to look to its distinctive features in order to be successful even in their own area. Economists, managers, planners, lawyers or biologists who claim to plan society from their own disciplinary standpoint are all guilty of reductionism, of ignoring the special features of a subject they have not studied for its own sake, but treat only as subordinate to their own schemes.

Going back to the analogy of the doctor and pharmacist; even if your sociologist is inadequate it is no answer to your dissatisfaction with society to turn to the manager, economist or lawyer. Better to rely on your common sense. It is not my argument that you turn to sociologists because they have all the answers, or to sociology because it is superior to any other trade. The point is that society is something in its own right.

Reductionism is the intellectual equivalent to cutting up the Bayeux tapestry to make use of the cloth or dismantling the Eiffel Tower to sell off the metal. Society has its own nature and sociologists are there both to study and protect it. This means being particularly vigilant, vigorous, assertive, but also co-operative when it comes to relations with other disciplines. But sociologists have to look to the defects of their own disciplinary outlook too.

Precarious humanity

Sociologists have often mistaken their own interest in society as being identical with a concern for humanity. So it may appear odd that they are often accused of treating human beings as if they were aliens. But there is some basis to this charge. Sociologists try to become as objective as possible about human society, which means treating the ordinary as strange. In everyday life people are not normally detached from familiar routines as they handle daily events. But sociologists need to be if they are going to treat the far off and foreign on equal terms with what is close to home.

But then they also seek to make the strange, ordinary; to relate it to, and build on, our past experience. The result is something neither everyday and familiar nor strange; neither for us nor for them; but newly understandable to both. If the job is done properly we enter a new world of knowledge, impersonal but accessible to anyone in the world.

The objective accessible strangeness of other worlds has become the playful theme of science fiction. At first glance science fiction is about imagined developments in science; just as often it is about the boundaries of humanity. Take a story like *Rendezvous with Rama* (1973) by Arthur C. Clarke.[26] It explores an imagined world which lays bare the assumptions on which we base our actual world.

It imagines the year 2131 when other planets have been colonised, asteroid-tracking systems have long been in place and a new entity appears unlike any other. A spacecraft is launched to land on the object, now named Rama, and meet the first visitors from the stars. It is an artefact, but with no sign of its builders. It looks brand new, but has to be older than anything on earth. Is it a cosmic Ark, sent to save the human race? Is it robot or spirit? It's more like a chemical processing plant than a city, and where are the Ramans? Eventually beings emerge with organic-metallic brains on legs. The scientists call them 'biots', electrically powered, with different forms for different functions, imitation living creatures.

The human inhabitants of the colonised Mercury conclude this is a non-biological survival of a technology far in advance of the human species. Its culture is so remote that co-operation with

165

it is as unlikely as it is with termites. They resolve to destroy it, but Rama proceeds without even noticing the human race – the ultimate insult.

There are two main fictional devices in the Rama story. The first is extrapolation, sketching a possible development for normal science within a historical narrative for the future. The second is a mythical deconstruction of our world. The new imagined entity, Rama, is an anti-world, revealing the fragility of the relations we rely on between biology, environment, human beings, and society.

What Clarke achieves in his story is a delinkage between history and humanity, whereby an entity which mimics human achievement, but betrays no human creator, removes history from people. History continues leaving people behind with no part to play. Clarke predicted the arrival of satellite communication, which puts him in the de Tocqueville class as a profound analyst of our time.[27] The Rama story is a parable of what may happen to humankind should it cease to promote the culture of humanity, and it makes it clear that we cannot take it for granted that it will do so.

Sociologists in particular need to judge how best society can serve the values of humanity and not take it for granted that the one equates with the other. We have to be objective about society; that means evaluating it in terms of human values. Objectivity entails freedom for values, not from them.

The way ahead

Scholars in classical China talked of the Way, Tao, as a guiding philosophy for human beings in a world which teaches us to find our own way. The idea of a Way is pervasive and important for human beings because it expresses the idea of passage over time and through space which is neither arbitrary nor erratic. It applies to both personal and collective life.

The idea of a Way in politics has great appeal currently after the end of the Cold War. The end of that period of global ideological power bloc politics is of course like neither side envisaged. The means to wage war are different from those needed to make a success of peace. Previously, for both sides the way ahead was the conquest of the other. The two alternatives were then pervaded by the sense of control and command, two rival systems of social power.

Once that contest is over there is no sense to providing some kind of compromise between them. No longer does anyone mobilise around capitalism and socialism. This is why there is a demand for a Way now, whereas previously neither of the opposing ideological camps were called 'ways'. They were quite literally battle positions, in a war of 'worlds': First, Second and Third Worlds. With the battle over we have 'North' and 'South' as symbolic rather than literal references to One World of vast inequalities of wealth. The 'Third World' belongs to the discourse of a past era.

The rival camps both strove to organise society and to mobilise its strengths for the great struggle. Two alternative principles dominated modernity and competed with each other to set the agenda for organising society. One was the state, coercion for a common good; the other the market, exchange on the basis of calculation of advantage. The former was the ancient Greek society, modernised as the nation-state, the latter took on the specifically modern form of world economy as society. But now that the drive to mobilise the two camps has ceased these two principles no longer appear to have the answers to the problems which face humankind.

This is why commentators have not been able to find the way in the 'Third Way', the title of two separate but not unrelated publications which appeared within a week of each other by British Prime Minister Tony Blair[28] and by sociologist Anthony Giddens.[29] They are straddling discourses of past and present. 'Third' evokes the conflict which is past, 'Way' suggests the present quest; but there are many, not just three, ways to follow.

One reason for the diversity of ways is that, without central control for the common cause, society's ever-potential autonomy challenges both state and economy. Harnessed to either, it makes them extra effective. Thus sociologists of ethnicity have been able to assist states following multicultural policies. Ethnicity is closer to being pure and naked social relations than either the state or the market, and it cross-cuts the boundaries of both in segmented labour forces. But ethnicity is not the only type of social relation. From friendship, to family, to voluntary associations, to global movements, the forces of society have a new zest for freedom from either state or market. But society is not the Third Way, although Bell once assigned voluntary and civic associations to a 'third sector' outside state and business.[30] The spatial allusion is apt. Society is the territory through which Ways have to be found.

The new freedom of society may be intoxicating for a time, but we are always bound to return to the problems of the life-world. Human social relations exist not for their own sake but for humankind, for individual people to live out their humanity. We can expect then the other life-spheres increasingly to demand an equal share with politics and economics in the setting of human goals. Culture and environment point to principles of free expression and of responsible reproduction which cannot be indefinitely suppressed without damage to humankind as a whole. Religion is radically opposed to the principles of both state and market in its concern for the sacred in life, and in creative tension with culture and environment.

Power itself, which can command all the life-spheres, is only a means to ends and must be subordinate to the satisfaction of human needs of all kinds, organised as they are in the life-spheres. Only in conflicts between collectivities does power come into its own as an overriding principle.

In brief, in the new Global Age in which we live there will be a plurality of ways in which human beings seek to find that balance between life-spheres which is appropriate to the new conditions. In finding that balance humankind is much more likely to find its collective interest if the right conditions for collectivities exist across the spheres. Since society is the condition for them all, and the goal of none, there must be a common interest in its nurture. Promoting the well-being of society is the way of ways.

If this account is true to the reality of our time then it expresses people's awareness already of a common interest across institutions and collectivities throughout the world. There is a common understanding of our collective interest in promoting free associations and tolerance and respect between them. This is a force which transcends political differences and the state itself mobilises to defend it when it is negated. When the denial of human rights and genocide affront the principles of free society, intervention by global state force, however constituted, in the affairs of nation-states becomes a necessary feature of the new common interest.

The role of the state in the new era must be to promote and defend free society, and the greatest honour will go to politicians who pursue the politics of and for free society. The way ahead is not state control of society, nor society without the state, but towards a state which supports society to generate purposes which go beyond them both. For that project we will need new global and local democratic institutions.

We also need sober assessment of the way society works under the new globalised conditions. The challenge to nation-state societies from globalisation arises from the autonomy it confers on associations of every kind. This is not primarily a matter of free markets and has little to do with border controls.

If we say that society now reappears as a *non-modern* reality this expresses the new strangeness which modernising governments must seek to understand. The state has now to adapt to the new society. Under these circumstances sociology is there to help governments, people and professionals to assess the new reality they have helped to make, but not in the ways they intended. This is the one small but important contribution sociology can make in assisting others to find common human purpose.

Note References

Preface

1   Herbert Spencer, *The Study of Sociology*, Henry King, London, 1873.

2   Fine examples for their time include Arthur Fairbanks, *Introduction to Sociology*, Scribner's, New York, 1896; Morris Ginsberg, *Sociology*, Oxford University Press, 1934; Alex Inkeles, *What is Sociology?*, Prentice Hall, Englewood Cliffs, N.J., 1964.

3   'Sociology's Saviour', *The Economist*, London, 12–18 August, 1998, p.32.

1   The nature of human society

1   For an account see Sanford M. Jacoby, *Modern Manors: Welfare Capitalism since the New Deal*, Princeton University Press, Princeton, N.J., pp. 172–74.

2   Adam Ferguson, *An Essay on the History of Civil Society*, Cadell, Creech and Bell, London and Edinburgh, 1767.

3   Ibn Khaldun, *The Muqaddimah: An Introduction to History*, translated by Franz Rosenthal, Routledge, London, 1958.

4   Richard W. Wrangham, W.C. McGrew, Frans B.M. de Waal and Paul G. Heltne (eds), *Chimpanzee Cultures*, Harvard University Press, Cambridge, Mass., 1994.

5   Edward Wilson, *Consilience: the Unity of Knowledge*, Knopf, New York, 1998, pp. 137–80.

6   Mary Wollstonecraft, *The Rights of Woman*, J.M. Dent, London, 1929, p. 5.

7   Jeff Hearn and Wendy Parkin, *'Sex' at 'Work': the Power and Paradox of Organization Sexuality*, Wheatsheaf, Brighton, 1987.

8   Edward Wilson, op. cit., p. 195.

9   Thorstein Veblen, *The Theory of the Leisure Class*, Huebsch, New York, 1899.

10   Joseph A. Schumpeter, *History of Economic Analysis*, Allen & Unwin, London, 1954, p.323.

11   Erving Goffman, *Asylums*, Anchor Books, New York, 1961.

12   Bruno Latour, *We Have Never Been Modern*, Harvester Wheatsheaf, Hemel Hempstead, 1993.

13   Norbert Elias, edited by Michael Schröter, *The Germans*, Polity Press, Cambridge, 1997, p. 147.

14   Arnold Toynbee, *A Study of History*, Volume 1, Clarendon Press, Oxford, 1935, pp. 442–43.

15   Edward Said, *Orientalism: Western Conceptions of the Orient*, Routledge, London, 1978.

16   Émile Durkheim, *The Rules of Sociological Method*, The Free Press, Glencoe, Ill., 1938, p. 110 (first French edition 1895).

17   Ulrich Beck, *Risk Society*, Sage, London, 1992.

18   Martin Albrow, *The Global Age: State and Society beyond Modernity*, Polity, Cambridge, 1996.

19   Herbert Spencer, *The Study of Sociology*, University of Michigan Press, Ann Arbor, 1961, p. 15.

20   James S. Coleman, *Foundations of Social Theory*, Harvard University Press, Cambridge, Mass., 1990, p. 301.

21   Nigel Gilbert and Rosaria Conte (eds), *Artificial Societies: the Computer Simulation of Social Life*, UCL Press, London, 1995.

2 The science of sociology

1   *The Republic of Plato*, translated by Francis Cornford, Clarendon Press, Oxford, 1941.

2   Pierre Bourdieu, *Homo Academicus*, Polity, Cambridge, 1988, p. 128.

3   Auguste Comte, *Cours de Philosophie Positive*, Bachelier, Paris, 6 vols, 1830–42, Vol. 4, p. 252.

4   William G. Sumner, *The Forgotten Man*, Yale University Press, New Haven, Conn., 1919, p. 405.

5   *American Journal of Sociology*, Vol. 1, No. 1, p. 1, July 1895.

6   Karl Marx, *Capital*, Vol. 1, Foreign Languages Publishing House, Moscow, 1954, pp. 444–46.

7   Peter Halfpenny, *Positivism and Sociology: Explaining Social Life*, Allen & Unwin, London, 1982.

8   Thomas S. Kuhn, *The Structure of Scientific Revolutions*, University of Chicago Press, Chicago, 1970.

9   W.G. Baldamus, *The Structure of Sociological Inference*, Martin Robertson, London, 1976.

10 D.J. de Solla Price, *Little Science, Big Science*, Yale University Press, New York, 1963.

11 G.D.H. Cole, *Social Theory*, Methuen, London, 1920, pp. 13–14.

12 Erving Goffman, *The Presentation of Self in Everyday Life*, Doubleday, New York, 1959.

13 Kai Erikson, *Sociological Visions*, Rowman and Littlefield, Lanham, Md., 1997, p.10.

14 Reuben Hersh, *What is Mathematics, Really?*, Cape, London, 1997.

15 Robert Reiner, Sonia Livingstone and Jessica Allen, 'Discipline or Desubordination? Changing Images of Crime in the Media since World War II', Paper presented to the 14th World Congress of Sociology, Montreal, 1998.

16 Robert S. Lichter, Linda S. Lichter and Stanley Rothman, *Prime Time: How TV Portrays American Culture*, Regnery Publishing, Washington, DC, 1994; Stephen P. Powers, David J. Rothman and Stanley Rothman, *Hollywood 's America: Social and Political Themes in Motion Pictures*, Westview Press, Boulder, 1996.

17 C. Wright Mills, *The Sociological Imagination*, Oxford University Press, New York, 1959, p. 195.

18 Eileen Barker, *The Making of a Moonie*, Blackwell, Oxford, 1984.

19 Ibid., p. 20.

20 Ibid., p. 121. The article appeared on 29 May 1978.

21   Commentaries on the Laws of England, Intr. 2.

22   R.W. Emerson, 'Self Reliance', in *Collected Works: Volume II, Essays First Series*, Belknap Press, Cambridge, Mass., 1979 (first edition 1841), p. 29.

23   Robert Michels, *Political Parties*, Collier Books, New York, 1962, p. 365.

24   Herodotus, *The Histories*, translated by Aubrey de Selincourt, Penguin, Harmondsworth, 1954, p. 190.

25   Michel de Montaigne, 'Of Custom, and that we should not easily change a law received', *Complete Works*, ed. by William Hazlitt, Templeman, London, [1580] 1842, p. 44.

26   Francis Bacon, 'Of Goodness and Goodness of Nature', in *Essays*, Grant Richards, London, [1625] 1902, p. 34.

27   Colin Bell and Howard Newby (eds), *Doing Sociological Research*, Allen & Unwin, London, 1977.

28   Written communication with the author. See also L. Radford and M. Hester, *Domestic Violence and Child Contact Arrangements in England and Denmark*, Policy Press, Bristol, 1996.

29   Address: 1722 North Street, NW, Washington, DC 20036, USA, e-mail executive.office@asanet.org

30   Address: Unit 39, Mountjoy Research Centre, Stockton Road, Durham, DH1 3UR, e-mail britsoc@dial.pipex.com

31   Address: Facultad C.C. Politicas y Sociologia, Universidad Computense, 228223 Madrid, Spain, e-mail isa@sis.ucm.es

32   Address: ESA, SISWO, Plantage Muidergracht 4, TV Amsterdam, Netherlands, e-mail kruithof@asanet.org

33   'The Forgotten Man' [1883], in William G. Sumner, op. cit., 1919, pp. 465–95.

34   Ann Oakley, *Subject Women*, Fontana, London, 1982, p. ix.

35   Sumner, op. cit., p. 492. Also (ibid.) 'It is plain that the Forgotten Man and the Forgotten Woman are the very life and substance of society.'

3   Sociological theory

1   Lewis H. Morgan, *Ancient Society*, Henry Holt, New York, 1977, p. 3.

2   Ferdinand Tönnies, *Community and Association*, Routledge, London, 1955.

3   Robert A. Nisbet, *The Sociological Tradition*, Heinemann, London, 1967, p. 74.

4 Amitai Etzioni, *The Spirit of Community*, Touchstone, New York, 1993.

5 William G. Sumner, *The Forgotten Man*, Yale University Press, New Haven, Conn., 1919, p. 403.

6 Martin Albrow, *The Global Age*, Stanford University Press, Stanford, 1997, pp. 85–90.

7 Norbert Elias, *The Civilizing Process*, 2 vols, Blackwell, Oxford, 1978–82.

8 Anthony Giddens, *Modernity and Self-Identity*, Polity, Cambridge, 1991, pp. 87–98.

9 Johann Wolfgang Goethe, *Faust*, Parts One and Two, translated by Robert MacDonald, Oberon, Birmingham, p. 51.

10 Max Weber, *Economy and Society*, edited by G. Roth and C. Wittich, University of California Press, Berkeley, 1978, p. 4.

11 Talcott Parsons, *The Structure of Social Action*, McGraw-Hill, New York, 1937.

12 Talcott Parsons, *The Social System*, The Free Press, Glencoe, Ill., 1951.

13 Alain Touraine, *Critique of Modernity*, Blackwell, Oxford, 1995, p. 209.

14 Émile Durkheim, *The Rules of Sociological Method*, The Free Press, Glencoe, Ill., 1938.

15 Émile Durkheim, *Suicide*, The Free Press, Glencoe, Illinois, 1951.

16 J. Douglas (ed.), *The Social Meanings of Suicide*, Princeton University Press, Princeton, 1967.

17 Robert Michels, *Political Parties*, Collier, New York, 1962.

18 Max Weber, op. cit., p. 53.

19 *The Times*, London, 4 June 1997, p. 5.

20 Max Weber, op. cit., pp. 20–21.

21 Alfred Schutz, *The Phenomenology of the Social World*, Northwestern University Press, Evanston, Ill., 1972.

22 Michel Foucault, *Discipline and Punish: the Birth of the Prison*, Vintage, New York, 1979.

23 Jürgen Habermas, *Theory of Communicative Action*, Polity, Cambridge, 1984.

24 Bronwen Maddox, 'Republicans fear Clinton video backlash', *The Times*, London, 18 September 1998, p. 1.

25 Marshall McLuhan, *Understanding Media*, Routledge, London, 1964, pp. 7–21.

26 Pitirim A. Sorokin, *Social and Cultural Dynamics*, Bedminster Press, Englewood Cliffs, N.J., 1937–41.

27   Robert Pirsig, *Zen and the Art of Motorcycle Maintenance*, Bodley Head, London, 1974, p. 403.

28   D. Lockwood, 'Social Integration and System Integration', in G.K. Zollschan and W. Hirsch (eds), *Explorations in Social Change*, Routledge, London, 1964.

29   Karl Popper, *The Open Society and its Enemies*, 2 vols, Routledge, London, 1945.

30   Adam Smith, *The Wealth of Nations*, Penguin, Harmondsworth, 1970, p. 119.

31   Stanley Milgram, *Obedience to Authority*, Tavistock, London, 1974.

32   Zygmunt Bauman, *Modernity and the Holocaust*, Polity, Cambridge, 1989.

33   Anthony Giddens, *The Constitution of Society*, Polity, Cambridge, 1984.

34   'Egyptian wife "can travel" ', *The Times*, London, 21 September 1998, p. 16.

35   Edward Said, *Orientalism*, Routledge, London, 1978.

36   Dennis H. Wrong, 'The Oversocialized Conception of Man in Modern Sociology', *American Sociological Review*, Vol. 26, 1961, pp. 183–93; reprinted in N.J. Demerath and R.A. Peterson (eds), *System, Change and Conflict*, Free Press, New York, 1967.

37   Francis Bacon, 'Of Goodness and Goodness of Nature', in *Essays*, Grant Richards, London, [1625] 1902, p. 34.

4   Social institutions

1   Herodotus, *The Histories*, translated by Aubrey de Selincourt, Penguin, Harmondsworth, 1954, p. 132.

2   Peter M. Blau, *The Dynamics of Bureaucracy*, University of Chicago Press, Chicago, 1955.

3   William G. Sumner, *Folkways: a Study of the Sociological Importance of Usages, Manners, Customs, Mores and Morals*, Mentor, New York, 1960.

4   Talcott Parsons, *The Social System*, The Free Press, Glencoe, Ill., 1951.

5   Bronislaw Malinowski, *The Dynamics of Culture Change*, Yale University Press, New Haven, Conn., 1945.

6   Dennis H. Wrong, 'The Oversocialized Conception of Man in Modern Sociology', *American Sociological Review*, Vol. 26, 1961, pp. 183–93,

reprinted in N.J Demerath and R.A. Peterson (eds), *System, Change and Conflict*, Free Press, New York, 1967.

7   James S. Coleman, *Foundations of Social Theory*, Harvard University Press, Cambridge, Mass., 1990.

8   Antonio Gramsci, *The Modern Prince and Other Writings*, International Publishers, New York, 1957.

9   Max Weber, *Economy and Society*, edited by G. Roth and C. Wittich, University of California Press, Berkeley, 1978, p. 54.

10 'Billions hidden offshore', *The Guardian*, 26 September 1998, p. 1.

11 Max Weber, *The Protestant Ethic and the Spirit of Capitalism*, Allen & Unwin, London, 1930.

12 Marshall Sahlins, *Stone Age Economics*, Tavistock, London, 1974, p. 55.

13 Raymond Firth, *Human Types*, Mentor, New York, 1958, p. 67.

14 Colin Turnbull, *The Mountain People*, Pan, London, 1974, pp. 193, 198.

15 Thorstein Veblen, *The Instinct of Workmanship*, Huebsch, New York, 1918.

16 Confucius, *The Analects*, translated by D.C. Lau, Penguin, Harmondsworth, 1979, p. 118.

17 Fred Hirsch, *Social Limits to Growth*, Routledge and Kegan Paul, London, 1977.

18 Ray Pahl, *Divisions of Labour*, Blackwell, Oxford, 1984.

19 Nico Stehr, *Knowledge Societies*, Sage, London, 1994.

20 Herodotus, op. cit., p. 110.

21 Émile Durkheim, *Selected Writings*, translated and edited by Anthony Giddens, Cambridge University Press, London, 1972, p. 88.

22 Émile Durkheim, *The Rules of Sociological Method*, The Free Press, Glencoe, Ill., 1938, p. 145.

23 Gro Harlem Brundtland, *Our Common Future: Report of World Commission on Environment and Development*, Oxford University Press, London, 1987.

24 Steven Yearley, *Sociology, Environmentalism, Globalization*, Sage, London, 1996.

25 Ulrich Beck, *Risk Society*, Sage, London, 1992.

26 Björn Jonasson (tr.), *The Sayings of the Vikings*, Gudrun, Reykjavik, 1992, p. 50.

27 *Oxford Dictionary of Quotations*, Book Club Associates, London, 1980, p. 4.

28   Anthony Giddens, *Modernity and Self-Identity*, Polity, Cambridge, 1991, pp. 17–18.

29   David Harvey, *The Condition of Postmodernity*, Blackwell, Oxford, 1989.

30   John Eade (ed.), *Living the Global City*, Routledge, London, 1997, p. 6.

31   Jörg Dürrschmidt, 'The Delinking of Locale and Milieu', in John Eade (ed.), op. cit., pp. 56–72.

32   E.B. Tylor, *Primitive Culture*, John Murray, London, 1871, p. 1.

33   Raymond Firth, *Elements of Social Organization,* Watts, London, 1951, p. 27.

34   A.L. Kroeber and C. Kluckhohn, 'Culture: A Critical Review of Concepts and Definitions', *Papers of the Peabody Museum of American Archaeology and Ethnology*, Vol. 47, No. 1, 1952, p. 181.

35   Paul Willis, *Learning to Labour*, Saxon House, Farnborough, 1977.

36   Georgina Born, *Rationalizing Culture: IRCAM, Boulez and the Institutionalization of Musical Avant-Garde*, University of California Press, Berkeley, 1995.

37   Charles Handy, *The Future of Work*, Blackwell, Oxford, 1985.

38   Sigmund Freud, *Introductory Lectures on Psychoanalysis*, Penguin, Harmondsworth, 1973.

39   George H. Mead, *Mind, Self and Society*, 3 vols, Chicago University Press, Chicago, 1934.

40   Norbert Elias, *The Civilizing Process*, 2 vols, Blackwell, Oxford, 1978–82.

41   Michel Foucault, *Discipline and Punish: the Birth of the Prism*, Vintage, New York, 1979.

42   Friedrich Nietzsche, *The Gay Science*, in *The Complete Works of Friedrich Nietzsche*, edited by Oscar Levy, Macmillan, New York and London, 18 vols, 1909–13.

43   Ruth Donner, *The Regulation of Nationality in International Law*, Societas Scientiarum Fennica, Helsinki, 1983.

44   Oliver E. Williamson, *The Economic Institutions of Capitalism*, The Free Press, New York, 1985.

5   Society in the future

1   Hugo Münsterberg, *The Americans*, McLure, Phillips, New York, 1904, p. 5.

2   Robert Owen, *The Life of Robert Owen*, Charles Knight, London, 1971, p. xxxvii.

3   H.H. Gerth and C.W. Mills, *From Max Weber*, Routledge, London, 1948, p. 139.

4   Peter Drucker, *Age of Discontinuity*, Harper & Row, New York, 1969; Daniel Bell, *The Coming of Post-Industrial Society*, Basic Books, New York, 1973; Nico Stehr, *Knowledge Societies*, Sage, London, 1994.

5   John Maddox, *What Remains to be Discovered*, Macmillan, London, 1998.

6   Ulrich Beck, *Risk Society*, Sage, London, 1992.

7   Robert K. Merton, 'The Unanticipated Consequences of Purposive Social Action', *American Sociological Review*, Vol. 1, 1936, pp. 894–904.

8   Richard Hofstadter, *Social Darwinism in American Thought*, University of Pennsylvania Press, Philadelphia, 1944.

9   Charles Darwin, *The Descent of Man*, 2nd edition, John Murray, London, 1874, p. 618.

10 Arnold Toynbee, *A Study of History*, 12 vols, 1934–61, Oxford University Press, London, Vol. V (1939), p. 638.

11 Adam Ferguson, *An Essay on the History of Civil Society*, Cadell, Creech and Bell, London and Edinburgh, 1767.

12 Jean-François Lyotard, *La Condition Postmoderne: rapport sur le savoir*, Les Editions de Minuit, Paris, 1979. (English edition: *The Postmodern Condition*, University of Minneapolis Press, Minn., 1984.)

13 C. Wright Mills, *The Sociological Imagination*, Oxford University Press, New York, 1959.

14 Herodotus, *The Histories*, translated by Aubrey de Selincourt, Penguin, Harmondsworth, 1954, p. 13.

15 Alexis de Tocqueville, *Democracy in America*, Harper, New York, pp. 412–13.

16 Samuel P. Huntington, *The Clash of Civilizations*, Simon and Schuster, New York, p. 42.

17 Ibid., p. 312.

18 Martin Albrow, *The Global Age: State and Society beyond Modernity*, Polity, Cambridge, 1996.

19 Sanford M. Jacoby, *Modern Manors: Welfare Capitalism since the New Deal*, Princeton University Press, Princeton, N.J., 1997.

20 Robert D. Putnam, *Making Democracy Work: Civic Traditions in*

Modern Italy, Princeton University Press, Princeton, N.J., 1994, p. 167.

21   Ivan Illich, *Medical Nemesis*, Calder and Boyars, London, 1975.

22   Daniel Bell, op. cit.

23   Alvin Toffler, *Future Shock*, Random, New York, 1970; *The Third Wave*, Bantam, New York, 1982.

24   Daniel P. Moynihan, 'Social Science and Social Policy: a Case Study of Overreaching', in Kai Erikson (ed.), *Sociological Visions*, Rowman & Littlefield, Lanham, Md., 1997, pp. 169–84.

25   Daniele Archibugi and David Held (eds), *Cosmopolitan Democracy*, Polity, Cambridge, 1995.

26   Arthur C. Clarke, *Rendezvous with Rama*, Gollancz, London, 1973.

27   Arthur Clarke, 'Extra-Terrestrial Relay', *Wireless World*, 1945, p. 305: 'A true broadcast service giving constant field strength at all times over the whole globe would be invaluable not to say indispensable, in a world society.'

28   Tony Blair, *The Third Way: New Politics for the New Century*, Fabian Society, London, 1998.

29   Anthony Giddens, *The Third Way: the Renewal of Social Democracy*, Polity, Cambridge, 1998.

30   Daniel Bell, op. cit., p. 269.

Further Reading

The following list is a selection of the fruits of sociology rather than the bare branches. It singles out items which are excellent reading, highly influential in the subject or controversial outside it.

Eileen Barker (1984) *The Making of a Moonie*, Oxford: Blackwell.

    The craft of the sociologist displayed to full effect in demystifying cult experience.

Zygmunt Bauman (1989) *Modernity and the Holocaust*, Cambridge: Polity.

    A savage indictment of modernity as tending to the rational production of evil.

Ulrich Beck (1992) *Risk Society*, London: Sage.

    The book which finally broke the mould of class analysis in post-war Germany and led the introduction of environmental concerns into sociological theory.

Daniel Bell (1973) *The Coming of Post-Industrial Society*, New York: Basic Books.

    Arguably the most important sociology book after 1945. Still unsurpassed for its scope and power as a forecast of the direction of contemporary society.

Robert N. Bellah, Richard Madsen, William M. Sullivan, Ann Swidler and Steven M. Tipton (1985) *Habits of the Heart: Individualism and Commitment in American Life*, New York: Harper & Row.
Fine example of the way focused interviewing with individuals can open up the widest consideration of the quality of contemporary society.

Stanley Cohen (1973) *Folk Devils and Moral Panics*, London: Paladin.
Pathbreaking account of collusion in the construction of presumed public menace between the media and deviant youth.

Norbert Elias (1985) *The Loneliness of Dying*, Oxford: Blackwell.
A giant of twentieth-century sociology reflects on the meaning of dying while in his mid-eighties.

Amitai Etzioni (1993) *The Spirit of Community*, New York: Simon and Schuster.
Powerful example of the political uses of sociology which has been highly influential in shaping the contemporary rhetoric of citizenship and personal responsibility.

Frantz Fanon (1961) *The Wretched of the Earth*, Harmondsworth: Penguin.
A firsthand account and key document for understanding the intellectual direction of revolutionary anti-colonial movements.

Anthony Giddens (1990) *The Consequences of Modernity*, Stanford: Stanford University Press.
The earliest book-length treatment of globalisation in sociology, marking a dramatic shift in the direction of this prolific and influential theorist of structuration.

Erving Goffman (1959) *The Presentation of Self in Everyday Life*, New York: Anchor.
Just one of many possible choices from the work of the most brilliant sociological writer of accounts of the mundane.

Arlie Hochschild (1983) *The Managed Heart: Commercialization of Human Feeling*, Berkeley: University of California Press.
Superb empirical sociological study of the capitalistic training of the happy faces of air crew.

Steven Lukes (1974) *Power: a Radical View*, London: Macmillan.
Just cool theory, a brief and incisive aid to finding power where it is also concealed.

C. Wright Mills (1959) *The Sociological Imagination*, New York: Oxford University Press.
Still worth looking at as the most important single inspirational statement of the purposes of professional sociology for the post-1945 generation of sociologists.

Jonathan Raban (1974) *Soft City*, London: Hamish Hamilton.

A free-ranging reconstruction of urban experience to fill in the gaps in expertly exploited standard sociological accounts.

Edward Said (1978) *Orientalism*, London: Routledge.

Already a classic, this is the key source for understanding the identity politics of ethnic minorities.

Richard Sennett (1980) *Authority*, New York: Knopf.

A radical revision of old orthodox thinking which takes the authority out of authoritarianism and paves the way for more human organisation.

Sue Sharpe (1976) '*Just Like a Girl': How Girls Learn to be Women*, Harmondsworth: Penguin.

Richly textured cross-section of girls' lives which beautifully lodges what they say in the context of media, schools and work.

Alvin Toffler (1980) *The Third Wave*, London: William Collins.

Pacy, superbly crafted, popular treatment of the consequences of technological change by a sociologist and opinion maker.

Paul Willis (1977) *Learning to Labour*, Farnborough: Saxon House.

A penetrating ethnographic study of young anti-school lads, long predating current concern for the crisis of male youth.

Michael Young and Peter Willmott (1957), *Family and Kinship in East London*, London: Routledge.

Possibly the most influential British sociological research report, both crystal clear and compelling.

Index

abortion 137
abstractions 58, 82, 88, 89; *see
    also* ideals; ideas; social
    relations; values
accounts 40, 41, 61, 62–3, 79,
    80; of institutions 95
action: collective 77, 100, 101;
    social 76; unplanned effects
    of 145
activities 7, 9, 37, 108, 110–11,
    157; collective 119;
    constructed and reconstructed
    95; economic 76; effects on
    environment 128; exclusively
    conducted 18–19; mental and
    manual, combination of 124;
    political party 117; private
    117; society the bearer of
    145; unanticipated
    consequences of 159;
    unplanned concentration and
    distribution 127

adaptability 6
affirmative action 95
age 51, 94, 95, 96, 98;
    adulthood 110
agency 72, 79
agriculture 124
alienation 87, 122, 142
Allen, Jessica 50–1
alliances 10, 25
ambiguities 110
America *see* United States
American Journal of Sociology
    34
American Sociological
    Association 63
Americanisation 20
Amnesty 162
analysis 11, 41, 44, 45, 51, 95;
    contemporary 81; unit of
    75–7
animal, social 112
animal, species 5, 6, 12, 163

anomie 104
anthropology 50, 52, 105, 122, 131, 134;
  one of the great founders 70
anti-social society 120
apartheid 95, 150
archaeology 52
argument 53, 56
Aristotle 69, 91, 112, 116
Aron, Raymond 64
artists 154
Asiatics 151
assimilation 71
association(s) 26, 43, 63, 72, 73, 100;
  autonomy conferred on 169;
  boundaries of 29–30; civic 168;
  concerted 149; ideas tarnished by 148;
  voluntary 35, 168
assumptions 75, 104, 105, 111, 120, 144;
  behaviour helps to create 135; laid
  bare 165; taken-for-granted 55
astronomy 78–9
attitudes 52
aural contact 89
authoritarianism 60
authority 52, 79, 90, 93, 112;
  demystification of 50; federal and
  overlapping 118; global 110;
  Weberian-style 94
autonomy 35, 62, 119, 159, 169; of
  culture 115, 131–5; social relations
  with a degree of 136
awareness 39, 101; global 22; see self-
  awareness

Bacon, Sir Francis 61
Bangladesh 66, 137
banking system 111
barbarism 12
Barker, Eileen 52–5
barriers 23

Bauman, Zygmunt 94
Beck, Ulrich 21, 128, 142
behaviour 83, 89; children's play 113;
  deviant 146; diversified within groups
  25; expectations 135; 'forcible' 85;
  interpersonal 136; norms of 44; other
  people judging 26; proper 9;
  'purchasing' 36; sexual 11; social 6,
  36; standards for 7; voting 36
beliefs 54, 58, 93, 136–7; dominant 12;
  shared 59
Bell, Daniel 161, 168
belonging 18, 44, 101
Berlin Wall 102
betrayal 59
bigots 97
biography 100, 101, 103
biology 6, 7, 8, 10, 11, 39, 41; complex
  organisms 148; origins of species 147;
  sociologists can't ignore 46;
  uniqueness 100; unit of analysis for 7
birth 136, 146, 160
black people 95
Blackstone, Sir William 57
Blair, Tony 65, 167
Blau, Peter 109
bodies 33, 100, 108, 136; socially
  constructed 101
bonds 97, 104, 139
Born, Georgina 132
Bosnia 97
Boulez, Pierre 132
boundaries 2–3, 18–19, 25, 26, 29–30;
  blurred 65–6; capital and religion 157;
  class 155; crossing 33, 43, 98, 104,
  130, 144; enclaves outside 120; gender
  125; group 25; identities and 99–105;
  national 97, 98; neatly coinciding 21;
  occupational 124; people and state
  have same 70; regional 97; sexual 11;

shifting 23; social activities 117; social relations 72; territorial 133
bourgeoisie 15, 120, 155
brainwashing 53, 54
breadwinners 47, 65
breeding 10, 148; selective 163
bribery 109
Britain 36, 50, 52, 66, 77, 111, 117; control of institutions 116; Labour Force Survey (1994) 46–7, 48; monarchy 111, 154; *see also* Blair; England; Scotland; Thatcher; Wales
British Sociological Association 63
Brundtland Report (1987) 127
buildings 19, 27, 115
bureaucracy 93, 94, 116

Canada 150
Capital (Marx) 15–16, 37, 71
capital 154, 158, 159, 160, 161; cultural 16, 126, 135, 156; global, power and 82; industrial dependence on 78; intensive farming 124; money and 13–17; ownership of 155, 161; personal 125–6; religion and 157; social relations of labour and 119
capitalism 4, 8, 9, 15, 36, 87, 95; bureaucracy 93; collapse of 44–5; future of 153–63; geared to the consumer 134; global interests 128; labour alienated under 122; organisation of 132; relation of intellectual life with 133; threat of 71; work predates 121
Carter, Jimmy 152
castes 74, 97
categorical imperative 60
categories 95
Catholic Church 111, 146
causality 126

causation 84
cause(s) 85, 88
centralisation 12
change 77, 94, 136; accounting for 145–53; ambivalence towards 88; biological 6, 7; boundaries subject to 3; continuing and partly self-induced 39; cultural 12, 13–14; desire to control 46; environmental 128; global 16; institutional 140; political 102; resistance to 80; retrenchment and 113; timespan of 46; understanding 86; *see also* social change
chaos 104, 110, 112
chemistry 75
Chernobyl 128
Chicago school 71, 127, 131
children 113, 123, 124, 125, 130; high cost of 145
chimpanzees 5
China 73, 74, 123, 128, 129, 152; classical, scholars in 166; Communist Party 64, 156; one-child policy 146; social order 147
choice 58, 77, 90, 151; career 66; conditions, opportunities and limits on 89; freedom of 6, 61, 75; individual 112; moral 40; *see also* rational choice
Christianity 70, 119, 144; fundamentalist 12; *see also* Protestants; Catholic Church
Christie, Agatha 42
churches 3, 4, 136, 137; *see also* Catholic Church; Moonies
Citizen Kane (Welles) 79
citizenship 23, 109, 149
city-states 69, 70
civil society theory 119, 149

civilisation(s) 12, 46, 70, 153; ancient 122, 124, 148; failure to respond to challenges 149; history of 152; large-scale 108
Clarke, Arthur C. 165–6
class *see* social class
classless society 80
cleavages 94, 96, 97, 99, 109; class 98; value 98
climate 126
Clinton, Bill 85–6
clubs 25
coalitions 25; female 5
coercion 79, 90, 92, 96, 110; neglected 111
cohabitation 84
Cold War (1945–89) 120, 152, 166
Coleman, James S. 112, 113
collaboration 45
collective bargaining 92
collectivities/collectives 3, 6, 7, 12, 13, 20, 40, 89; action 77; activities subordinated to 111; central 163; changing 23; gene pools and 148; institutions and 17–19, 107–8, 109; justification of standard practices 59; sectors of experience which pervade 114–38; survival of 111
common life 91
common sense 86, 164
communal living 71
communication 6, 25, 84–5, 89; breadth and scope reduced 99; equal 97; free 39, 97; global 156; most intense 86; satellite 166; technical advances 88; world-wide 130
communism 64, 87, 120, 156; victory over 161
communitarianism 64–5, 72

communities 19, 43–4, 59, 78, 81, 121; alliances between 10; exclusive, territorially based 5; ideal 143; local 72, 74; loss of 142; organisation of 16; persistent call for return to 104; political 73, 92; rural 71; territorially based 69, 129
competition 124, 148
competitiveness 9, 92
compliance 115
computers 89, 124
Comte, Auguste 32, 34, 37, 144, 149, 150
concepts 23, 28, 45, 74, 83; as aids to understanding 147; crucial 148; in research 43–9
conceptualisation 44, 45, 83
confidence 103, 142
conflict 50, 54, 62, 79, 110, 151; class 22; cleavage does not necessarily mean 97; employers and trade unions 90; family 98; group 92; ideological 120; institutionalised 120; interpersonal 125; inter-state 120; neglected 111; no-holds-barred 104; social 135
conformity 57
Confucian theory 74, 123
connections 2; foreign 3
conscience 60, 136
consciousness 37, 45, 66, 74, 130; collective 21; revival of 129
consensus 89, 112
conservatives/conservatism 87, 113
consolidation 38
constraint 42, 86
construction 27–30; continuous 95; *see also* social construction
consumption 35, 36, 87, 88, 155; conspicuous 14, 134
context 77

contraceptives 11, 144, 146
control 3, 22, 25, 36, 45, 79, 96, 167;
    central 89, 146; continuous expansion
    of 23; desire to 46; impersonal 88;
    institutional 116; loss of 88; media 82,
    85; nature 142, 156; resistance to 143;
    rights to 115; social practices resistant
    to 17, 27; state 71, 100–1, 116–17,
    119, 120; threat to get out of 80; *see
    also* social control
control freaks 143–5
conurbations 71
conversations 53; telephone 89
co-operation 48, 50, 90, 91–2, 96, 119;
    minimal 122; possibilities of 104;
    world-wide 13
corporations 4, 154; global/transnational
    3, 160, 162
corporatism 120
'corruption' 91
countries 19, 20–1, 101; poor 103; *see
    also* nation-states
courage 14
craftsmanship 122; intellectual 52–5
Crick, Francis 38
crime 50–1, 52, 93; reporting 135
criticism 80, 83
critiques 40, 87, 88; feminist, of
    objectivity 62; ideology 59; pessimistic
    nostalgia in 89; power and 77–80
cronies 162
crowds 26, 155
cults *see* Moonies
'cultural dopes' 76
culture(s) 21, 43, 73, 98, 105, 168;
    ancient, ravages of Western civilisation
    on 122; autonomy of 131–5; changes
    in 12, 13; contrasting 57; different,
    tolerance of 104; humankind and 5–8,
    100; language and 6, 9, 20; modern

global effects on 99; remote 165–6;
    sexuality and 9, 10, 11; sharing 20;
    social relations mediated through 59;
    society and 14, 38
currency *see* money
curriculum 66
customs 59, 119, 151; sexual 60

dark-skinned people 95
Darwin, Charles 71, 147, 149
data 46–7, 52; 'hard' 38; models tested
    against 58–9; officially gathered 40;
    systematic gathering of 69
databases 75
deals 88
death 136, 146, 160
de Tocqueville, Alexis 151–2
decentralisation 12
decision making 45; investment 160
democracy 12, 58, 116, 120, 136;
    attempts to limit 156; 'cosmopolitan'
    162; de Tocqueville's study of 151;
    'shareholder' 156
demography 37, 145
Deng Xiaoping 64
dependence 17, 24, 88, 100, 147; mutual
    4, 8
deprivation 95
desires 46, 78, 111, 112
determinism 133; geographical 126
development 147; self 136; stages 12
deviance 107, 110, 111, 146
dialogue 86, 100
difference 7, 52, 82, 99–101; class 45,
    51, 96; custom 60; gender 51, 96;
    individual, reality of 103; sexual 8, 9;
    social 77
dignity 75, 110
dilemmas 60, 86, 90; famous 78; moral
    57

disadvantages 48, 95

discourse 85, 160, 167; metaphorical 42, 43; paradigms and 37–41

discrimination 48

dismantling 12

disorder 71

distance 62–3, 89; ritual 97

distribution 127; unequal 14

diversity 26, 52, 60, 62, 84; cultural 111, 132; household and family arrangements 125; sectional interests 116

division of labour 69, 92, 124; domestic 125; social 119; world-wide 70

divisions 24, 63, 94, 95, 97, 151; class 115; political 129; religious 70; *see also* division of labour

divorce 98, 117

doctrine 54

drama 42, 43, 152

drives 112

Durkheim, Émile 22, 52, 66, 77, 97, 127, 149; suicide study 77, 126

dynamics 77, 113

dynasties 162

earnings 47–8, 125

Eastern Europe 162

Eastern Tigers 123

ecology 127

economic growth 22, 74

economics 8, 15, 33, 35, 38, 41, 50, 64; development of 76; models tested against data 58–9; new institutionalism 121, 139; political economy developed into 70; purely rational agent 83; sociologists can't ignore 46; sociology closer to 52; technical interest in 92

education 14, 23, 35, 66, 114, 116; individual chances 135; long and arduous 123; politics of 135; poor 48; popular 34; population growth and 146

'effective link' 139

efficiency 9, 94

efforts 6–7, 80, 122

egalitarianism 12

Egypt 99, 108, 148

Einstein, Albert 38

Elias, Norbert 21, 74, 136

elites 36, 71, 98

e-mail 89

Emerson, Ralph Waldo 57

empiricism 41

employers 90, 120, 155; moving between 134

employment *see* work

enactments 88

enemies 23

energy 10, 57, 160

Engels, Friedrich 154

England 111

Enlightenment 79

environment 8, 114, 121, 159, 160; collective relations with 22; complex engagements with 13; damage to 116; global risk 126–31; irreversible effects on 147

equal opportunities 9, 109

equality 10, 39, 48, 74, 77, 80, 90; coerced 92; considered in a mathematical sense 82; degree necessary for common humanity to prevail 94; flouted 108; meaning of, in nature and society 81; perfect 143

'establishments' 19

esteem 99

ethics 62, 63; medical 57, 108; Protestant 123

ethnicity 95, 97, 121, 161, 162, 167

ethnocentrism 109

ethnography 50, 52
ethology 49
etiquette 110
Etzioni, Amitai 65
eugenics movement 148
European Court of Justice 117
European Sociological Association 63
evidence 51, 54, 62
evil 93, 94
evolution 6, 7, 148; controversy on 137; history and 11–13, 147, 148; unpredictability of 152
exchange 17, 84, 90, 96; mutual 162; of ideas 34, 39; peaceful 92; product 119
exclusion 96, 97
Exodus 122
expenditure 14
experience 13, 38, 43, 55, 114–38; development of 113; diversity of 62; primary 61, 77; shared 82; survivors' accounts of 63
explanation 36, 46–9, 52; causal 76
exploitation 95, 110, 157
exploration 44
expressions 84, 100, 103, 154; unavoidable 31
externalities 74

facticity 77, 78
factories 15, 87, 115
facts 40, 54, 60; approaches to 55; gathering 41; measured 81; social 77, 126
faith 138, 141, 143; blind 142
fallacies 11–12
family 4, 24, 56, 83–4, 87, 125, 145; conflicts in 98; individuals in 73; interaction of members 136; planning 146; politics 49, 96; threat to 53
farming 124, 130

fascism 85, 120, 156; victory over 161
'Faust' (Goethe) 76, 77
Fei Xiaotung 64
feminism 10, 62
Ferguson, Adam 4, 92, 119, 149
fetish 10
feudal society 153–4
films 50, 51
finance 16, 88
first principles 79
Firth, Raymond 122
fluidity 26
force 118, 135
Foucault, Michel 39, 40, 79, 85, 136
France 22, 71; Revolution (1789) 74, 80, 119–20
fraternity 75, 80, 81, 82, 97
free will 58
freedom 39, 59–62, 75, 76, 84, 89, 166; collective 6; constraint on 86; ever-advancing 150; implicit 85; new zest for 168
Freud, Sigmund 11, 135
Friends of the Earth 129, 162
friendship 4, 59, 139
functionalism 110–11
fundamentalism 12
future 141–69; modernity's outlook on 87; new, creation of 71

Gaulle, Charles de 64
Gemeinschaft und Gesellschaft (Tönnies) 71
gender 94, 95, 97, 124, 125; definitions 98; differences 51, 96; institutions to regulate 110; sex and 8–11
gene–culture coevolution 6
genes/genetic factors 6, 33, 148; defects 10; inheritance 7
'geographical determinism' 126

German Sociological Association 56
Germany 20, 71; Social Democratic
    Party 77; unification of 102; *see also*
    Nazis
gestures 86
Giddens, Anthony 65, 74, 95, 96, 167
Global Age, The (Albrow) 23, 96, 153,
    168, 172n18, 175n6, 179n18
global issues 4, 21–3, 99, 103, 160, 166;
    change 16; communications 156;
    family planning 146; human rights law
    118; interdependence 153; intervention
    by state force 168; new authorities
    110; power 20, 82; risk 13, 126–31;
    sexual identity 8
global warming 17, 22, 128
globalisation 17, 20, 72–4, 96, 129, 169;
    discourse of 160; economic, forces of
    130; 'from below' 162; paradoxical
    consequences 161–2; personal identity
    and 101
God 56, 79; existence of 137; persons
    and 135–8
Goethe, J. W. von 76, 77
Goffman, Erving 19, 42, 43, 50
goodness 61
Gorbachev, Mikhail S. 64
governments 37, 40, 96, 99, 150, 160;
    sociology there to help 169
Gramsci, Antonio 115
grand narrative 11, 101, 103, 149–53,
    159; world 160
Greece/Greeks 4, 35, 39, 70, 71, 75, 79,
    88, 158; direct democracy 12;
    modernised as nation-state 167; wars
    between Persians and 151; *see also*
    Aristotle; Herodotus; Plato; Socrates
Green movement 26, 73
Greenpeace 129
gross national product 120

grounded theory 41–2
groups 43, 69, 91–2, 135; behaviour
    diversified within 25; campaigning
    162; caste 74; focus 51; interest 98;
    knowledge-based 162; membership of
    25, 26–7, 53, 102, 103, 134; relations
    between 10; religious 53, 55, 136;
    societies' expectations of 129;
    Trotskyite 137; watchdog 116
guilt 135

Habermas, Jürgen 39–40, 85, 88
Haeckel, Ernst 127
Handy, Charles 134
happiness 141
harassment 62, 63
harm 93
Harvey, David 130
hazards 62, 142; environmental 128
health 14, 103, 108, 116, 136, 164;
    liberal concern for 147; policies
    promoting 146
hegemony 79, 115
Herodotus 59–60, 101, 126, 151,
    152
Hersh, Reuben 50
hierarchy 94; values 14
Hindus 97
Hiroshima 22
history 40, 52, 79, 102, 133, 143, 152,
    166; determined by technology 89;
    evolution and 11–13, 147, 148;
    intellectual 132; laws of 150, 151;
    Marx's theory 44; materialistic
    conception of 154; present time and
    146; subordination of 144, 150
Holocaust 93, 94
Homer 103
hostility 32, 33, 34, 52, 53, 97
households 19, 47

human association 18, 24, 25–7
human capital 16
human existence 7, 17, 22, 88, 127,
    142
human rights 61, 109, 139, 145; denial
    of 168; law 118
human species 5, 11, 21, 100, 143, 144,
    165; adaptability of 5–6
humanity 5, 7, 21, 80, 94, 105, 154, 155,
    157–9, 162, 165–8
humankind 5, 13, 17, 21, 23, 70, 72, 75,
    78, 80, 84, 93, 100–3, 126–9, 142,
    147, 159, 166–8
Huntington, Samuel 152
'hybrids' 19
hypotheses 47

Ibn Khaldun 4
ideal types 81–4, 89
idealism 104, 143
ideals 61, 78, 140; abstract 60
ideas 45, 59, 75, 82, 102, 134, 144;
    abstract 154; clash of 133;
    communication of 6; connection of 41;
    core 143; developing 42; embodied in
    technology 87; exchange of 34, 39;
    familiar 83; popular 45; power
    operating through 115; production of
    39; pure 83; reality and 79; religious
    133; sharing 39, 88; tarnished by
    association 148
ideation 86, 87, 89
identification 97
identity 73; boundaries and 99–105;
    occupational 35; professional 64;
    sexual 8–9
ideology 12, 78, 79–80, 89, 111, 133;
    conflicts 120; global power-bloc
    politics 166; imperialist 122;
    objectivity and 56–9; 'one communal

pot' 64; oppositional 115; professional
    35; social 121; sociological theory of
    62
ignorance 141–3, 152
Illich, Ivan 160
images 83; 'iron cage' 123; oriental 102;
    self- 102
inbreeding 10
incentives 48
incest: institutionalised 148; taboo 10, 26
incidence 136
inclusion 96, 97
income 14–15, 111
independence 17, 23, 42, 82, 125, 133;
    economic, policies promoting 146
India 73, 74
individualisation 7, 17, 100; apathetic 88;
    ever-increasing 113
individualism/individuality 92, 101
individuals 23, 56, 57, 72–3, 75–6;
    existence of 112; mobilisation of
    people as 88
industrialisation 136
industry 15; decline of 130
inequality 81, 82, 90, 109, 167; consent
    to 92–3; counter to 91
inferences 52, 85
inflation 16
information 39, 52, 54; analysing 46;
    excluding people from 85; gathering
    50, 89; public 49
information technology 88, 130, 140
informed consent 85
infrastructure 16
inheritance 7, 148
inhumanity 7, 158
insecurity 125, 128, 144; childhood 79;
    ontological 103, 104
inspiration 88, 115
instability 160

institutionalisation: citizenship 109; conflict 120; gassing 148–9; incest 148; pursuit of knowledge 162–3

institutions 16, 20, 25, 26, 85, 107–40; accounts of 95; and collectivities 17–21; existence of 110–12; global and local democratic 169; law-abiding 3; mass media 82; political 153; rational 76; servants of 159; *see also* institutionalisation

insurance 160

integration 72; national 97; social 52, 104; system 88

intellectual issues 33, 37, 62, 79, 83, 132, 133, 142; craftsmanship 52–5; curiosity 46; order 32; strategy 58

intellectual property 16

intentions 86

interaction 23, 39, 53, 83, 90, 113, 129; family members 136; intensity increased 149; meaning of 43; social 105

interdependencies 130, 153

international relations 3

International Sociological Association 63

Internet 86, 89

interpretation 57

'interpretative' approach 55

intervention 46, 81; state 119, 168

invention 78, 142

'invisible colleges' 39

Ireland 117; Northern 97

Israelites 122

Italy 66

Japan 123

Jews 70, 72, 93, 102; gassing of 148

jobs *see* occupations; work

judgements 55; legal 99, 108, 117

justice 77, 118

Kahn, Herman 160

Kant, Immanuel 60

kinship 70

Klimt, Gustav 11

knowledge 33, 36, 37, 46, 47, 143; application of 39; based on universal truth 59; contemporary state of 150; limits of 152; new world of 164; public 107; universality of 162

knowledge society 126, 142

Kuhn, Thomas 38

labour 14, 87; alienated under capitalism 122; domestic 125; factories worthless without 15; mental and manual 124; social relations of capital and 119; *see also* division of labour; labour market disadvantage

labour market disadvantage 48

language 40, 41, 84; culture and 6, 9, 20; everyday 31, 45; grammar 86; shared 100; syntax 28; vocabulary 86, 100

Latour, Bruno 19

law 3, 35, 50, 52, 60, 85, 114, 124; behavioural expectations built into 135; developing 61; duty to uphold 92; human rights 118; institutions and 109–10; interplay of society and 86; marriage 139; recognises individuals 75

lawyers 83, 91

laziness 122

learning 18, 28; lifelong 65–7

legitimacy 92, 118

leisure class 122

Leviathan (Hobbes) 112

Lewinsky, Monica 85

liberty 14, 74, 80, 81, 89

life-chances 45

life-spheres 17–18, 114–15, 119, 134, 138, 139, 146, 168

lifestyle 36, 73, 155
light-skinned people 95
linguistics 38, 41
listening 53
Livingstone, Sonia 50–1
location 91
Locke, John 134
logic 82, 83, 134, 137, 154
London 42, 89
London School of Economics 64, 65
Lord of the Flies (Golding) 112, 113
love 56, 90, 129, 143; making 85, 86
Lyotard, Jean-François 150, 160

McLuhan, Marshall 86
Mafia 162
male dominance/domination 5, 10, 40
Malinowski, Bronislaw 110
manners 110, 119
market research 36–7
markets 10, 14, 24, 45, 70, 78; accounts
    of 79; basis of 104; co-operation in
    92; failure of 116; 'free' 89; global
    103; job 63; mass 11; pure 94; *see
    also* labour market
marriage 27, 84, 98, 136; mixed 97;
    partnerships outside 139; regulation of
    99
Marx, Karl 66, 91, 112, 115, 120, 140,
    149, 152; alienated labour 122; class-
    divided society 158; collapse of
    capitalism 44–5; historical materialism
    119, 126, 133; power of social classes
    79; social relations 74, 78, 87; society
    and capital 15–16, 36, 37, 71, 154
Marxism 98, 115, 127, 133
masses 120, 124
material things 17, 56, 89
materialism 119, 126, 133, 154
mathematics 49–50, 58, 82, 83

maturation 6
Mead, G. H. 136
meaning 21, 27, 43, 59, 60, 77, 81,
    136; deep 86; social relations learned
    and conducted within frames of
    131–2
measurement 51, 52, 81, 108
mechanics 88
media 52, 84, 88, 129, 152; control of
    82, 85; mass 82, 89, 91, 103, 134; *see
    also* films; press; television
mediation 53, 59, 81, 84–90
medicine 35, 39, 57, 108, 113, 124, 160;
    sociology of 136
membership *see* groups
memory 151; collective 40, 155
men 9, 56; employment 46–7, 48; equal
    rights for 125
Merton, Robert 142
metaphor 131–2, 142; theory and 41–3
methods *see* research
Michels, Robert 77
Middle Ages 151
middle classes 11, 108
migration 103
Milgram, Stanley 93, 94
mind 33, 76; growth of 150; 'raped' 54;
    sane, persons of 135
minorities 55
misunderstanding 44, 45, 123
models 58–9, 83
Modern Age 22–3, 141, 143, 155–6;
    revolutions 157; society before 158
modernisation 156
modernity 12, 70, 80, 87, 94, 143,
    158; key feature of 71; most
    important collective force of 82;
    self-image of 122; specialisation
    not a result of 108
monarchy 111, 116

money 111, 125; and capital 13–17; saving and borrowing 155; social relations mediated by 88

Montaigne, Michel de 60

Montreal 63

Moonies 52–5

morality/morals 57, 59, 60, 62, 80, 110; diversity of 60; universal 61, 104

Morgan, Lewis 70, 87

motivation 111, 123, 124

movement 2, 26; free 135

movements 76; *see also* Amnesty; communitarianism; eugenics movement; Friends of the Earth; Green movement

Moynihan, Daniel P. 161

mujahedin 137

multicultural society 161, 167

Murdoch, Rupert 82

musical avante-garde 132

Muslims 70, 144

'mythological proper persons' 21

names 21

narrative 40, 41, 150; historical 87; *see also* grand narrative

nation-states 3, 4, 16, 20–3, 28–30, 169; apex of institution building 110; citizenship institutionalised in 109; counterweight to 119; elites controlling 71; leaders of 158–9; modern, state in 116–17; ordering within 70; overriding interest of governments 37; parameters of society fixed by 96; problem of integration into 72; regarded as only real state 117–18; ruling elites 36; solidarity of 97, 162; Weber's classic definition 118; Western, Great War between 34

nationalism 57, 97, 133; imperialistic 118

nationality 3, 96, 101, 102; right to 139; shared 20

Native Americans 70

'natural selection' 148

nature 19, 60, 81, 127, 147, 149; ability to control 142; relations to 157; work, human beings and 119

Nazis 16, 36, 94, 150; gassing institutionalised by 148–9

needs 110, 112, 113, 158; customer 115; emotional 87; nation-states measured by 23; satisfaction of 111; work for 119–26

neo-institutionalism 112

networks 12, 162; social 39

neurosis 135

New York 89

New Zealand Maoris 122

newspapers 50, 51, 54

Nietzsche, Friedrich 137

norms 39, 59, 76, 104, 107; ambivalent 7; individuals demand 112; set by workers 109; shared 44

North Korea 53

nuclear reactors 128

nutrition 111

Oakley, Ann 65

obedience 93; unquestioning 94

objectivity 54, 61, 77, 166; feminist critique of 62; ideology and 56–9; positivist view of 81

objects 10, 13, 49, 56, 63, 82; comparing 14; defining and sorting 77; hate 83; hybrid 19; ideal, production of 119; made and sold 87; material 119, 126; processes and 27

observation 50, 51, 57, 79, 145; participant 53, 54

occupations 35, 94; distinct, growth of
   119; divided by status 95; gender
   divide 124; industrial 37; service 121,
   124; specialised 92, 124
oligarchy 58, 77, 116
opinions 51, 54; *see also* public opinion
opposition 115, 121
order 7, 74; bourgeois 120; institutional
   119; intellectual 32; law and 50; status
   123–4; time 86; *see also* social order
organisation(s) 19, 24, 79, 90, 127;
   authority in 94; capitalist 132; collective
   12; community 16; consequences
   for working of 140; democratic 58;
   ideal 109; 'informal' 109; large,
   concentration of power in 77;
   non-governmental, transnational 118;
   professional 129; rational 71; sexuality
   and 10; *see also* social organisation
oriental images 102
output 115, 116
overthrow 38
Owen, Robert 141

pacification 149
Pahl, Ray 47, 125
paradigms 37–41
parents 47, 86, 98; anxious 53;
   imposition of norms on children 113;
   outraged 54; responsible 101
Parsons, Talcott 42, 72, 76, 110, 112
participation 25, 53, 108, 150
partnerships 27, 84, 120; outside
   marriage 139
patriarchy 9, 12
peasants 45, 123, 129, 157
performance 28, 42, 43, 55
permissiveness 11
'personal Odyssey' 103
phenomena 147

philosophy 32, 43
physical contact 86
physics 37, 38, 75
Plato 33, 69, 80
play behaviour 113
plays 42
pleasure 136
police 50–1, 109
political correctness 12
political economy *see* economics
politics 3, 8, 9, 33, 37, 51, 64, 80, 133;
   capitalism and 156; education 135;
   environmental 127; family 49, 96;
   highly charged topic 57; identity 102;
   international changes 102; liberalising
   regimes 11; movements 83; power-bloc
   166; sociology of 36; world 152
Popper, Sir Karl 88
population 137; census 37; growth 143,
   145–6, 149, 153, 160
positivism 37–8, 40, 81
'positivist' approach 55
post-Fordist era 121
'postmodern condition' 150, 159
poverty 96, 137
power 36, 82, 102, 136, 168; absolute
   112; balance of 90, 121;
   communication and 85; creative 9;
   critique and 77–80; defined 78;
   equalisation of 85; global 20; operating
   through ideas and everyday practices
   115; political 98; purchasing 14; social
   15, 167; state 117, 118; tension with
   84; terms of discourse established
   through 40
practices 18, 19, 25, 39; enforcement 117;
   everyday, power operating through 115;
   institutional(ised) 107, 110, 111, 113,
   116, 121, 148–9; social 17, 27, 38;
   standard(ised) 59, 107, 113; working 121

pragmatism 60–1
preference 117
prejudice 53, 92, 93, 102, 103
press 54; *see also* newspapers
prestige 44
prices 14
privileges 45
problems 72, 161; social 96, 97; universal 146–7
processes 52, 136; objects and 27
production: agricultural 64; dependent on social relations of capital and labour 119; disruption to 120; of material and ideal objects 119; means of 45; social relations of 74, 78, 87
professionalism 62–5
prohibitions 40, 135
propaganda 89
properties 75, 95
Protestants 121, 123
proverbs 122
psychoanalytic theory 11
psychology 35, 38, 50, 52, 64, 135
public goods 20
public opinion 36
purchasing: behaviour 36; power 14
Puritans 123

qualifications 124, 155
questionnaires 51, 54

racism 95, 109, 161; Nazi 148
Radford, Lorraine 62–3
radicals 87, 89, 114, 119
Rand Corporation 160
rational choice 24, 41, 76; institutions and 110
rationalisation 142
rationality 9, 76, 94; everyday 83; pure 83
reading 76

reality 28, 41–5, 55, 62, 83, 85, 159; application of reason to 79; autonomous 62; conceptual 52; day-to-day 121; group membership 102; individual differences 103; lack of confidence in 103; non-modern 169; science and 31–4; social relations 83, 84; test of 58; understanding world society as 153; virtual 130; woven into lives of people 4; *see also* social reality
reason(ing) 79, 82, 148
reconstruction 12, 13, 40
reductionism 163–9
reflexivity 39, 46
regularities 94, 118
regulation 99, 110; state 115, 116
Reiner, Robert 50–1
relations/relationships 17, 28, 84; collective 22; competitive 92; complexity of 127; enduring 44; ever-changing 157; everyday knowledge of 59; gender 8, 9; ideational 86, 89; individual–society 72; industrial 109, 121; institutions to regulate 110; international 3; interpersonal 74, 91, 96, 97, 119; intimate 26; men and women 47; political 3; power 9; reflexive 7; self-expression in 40; sensate 86, 88; sexual 27, 85; society-society 72; technical 89; *see also* social relations
relativism 60
religion 14, 53, 55, 59, 60, 74; capital and 157; Darwin on 148; dogma, schism and heresy in 137; opposition to state and market 168; science and 137–8; society pushed out by 87; sociology of 136; *see also* Christianity; Jews; Muslims

Rembrandt 84

reproduction 8, 94, 168; key institutions concerned with 111

research 28, 30, 32, 34, 62, 73, 81, 82; guiding criteria for 80; lifestyle 36; market 36–7; media-related 64; methods of 41–55, 66; moral courage in 63; population 145; social 36; theory and 69

resistance 17, 27, 78, 79, 80, 95

resources 33, 69, 127, 158; business and state 40; common 100; control of 14–15; depletion and exhaustion of 128; material 113; religion exploited as 157; scarce, conflict over 92; world population growth and 145

respect 99, 110, 115; mutual 94

responsibility 75, 76, 93, 135; personal 72, 104

'responsibility system' 64

revolutions 5, 157; see also France; Russia

rewards 111

rights 115; animal 137; civil 130; denying 78; equal, for men 125; historic 117; nationality 139; ownership of 16; power to assert 117; voting 135; women's 10, 62, 146; see also human rights

Rio Earth Summit (1992) 129

risk 64, 142; global 126–31

risk society 21, 128, 172n17, 177n25, 179n6

rituals 123

roles 42, 53; state 119, 169

rules 94; breaking 109; government 99; social relations 61; stabilisation functions of 139; see also norms

ruling classes 16, 79

Russia 102, 152; Revolution (1917) 80, 120

sado-masochism 117

Sahlins, Marshall 122

Said, Edward 22, 102

St John's gospel 76

sanctions 107

savagery 12

savings 16

scenarios 159–63

Scheler, Max 59

schism 137

Schutz, Alfred 83

science 45, 76, 78, 79, 80–1, 94; applied, blind faith in 142; belief in 136; dependence on 147; history and 147; history of 38–9; reality and 31–4; religion and 137–8; sociology as 31–67, 126; see also biology; chemistry; physics

science fiction 164

Scotland 111

Second World War 93, 156, 161

sects 136; see also Moonies

secularisation 137

security 111, 159; ontological 138

self-awareness 11

self-defence 135

self-determination 75

self-discipline 123

self-expression 40

self-interest 92, 110

self-realisation 7

self-sufficiency 125

selfishness 122

servant class 37

sex/sexual matters 40; abstinence 146; customs 60; definitions 98; difference 96; gender and 8–11; relationships 27, 85; repression 135

sexism 49, 109

Shakespeare, William 42

Shell 160
shelter 111
signs 86, 134
Simmel, Georg 72, 92, 131, 132
slaves 71
Small, Albion 34
Smith, Adam 92, 119, 120
smokestack industries 121, 124
social change 53, 139, 144; cumulative 147
social class 37, 44–5, 46, 73, 94, 116, 130; capitalist 155; cleavage 98; conflict 22; differences 45, 51, 96; divisions 115; interests 120, 133; interests overlooked 111; power of 79; struggle 142; *see also* middle classes; ruling classes; servant class; working classes
social construction 32, 40, 55; bodies 101
social control 115; relaxed 11
social order 16, 50, 144, 147; crisis of 22; source of 70, 92–3
social organisation 70; simpler types replaced 149; state control of 120
social reality 46, 51, 61
social relations 5, 7, 8, 19, 23–5, 30, 35, 77, 80; abstraction of 123, 130; aggregate set of 131; autonomy of 115; bonded into entities 13; boundaries for 72; candidates for accounting 158; capital and labour 119; capital in terms of 161; changing 61, 110; cognitive frame for communicating 62; condition which pervades 52; configurations of 72, 161; constellations of 71, 73, 91, 116, 136; crucial for countries' maintenance 21; defined exclusively by power and communication 85;

dependence on 100; extension of 126; features affecting 143–4; features which hide behind presentation 109; first-order 95, 97, 139, 145, 146; foregrounded 74; frame for 104; fundamental 92; importance of discourse in 40; institutions and 18, 110, 113, 139; interpersonal 120; lateral 94; learned and conducted within frames of meaning 131–2; locatedness of 129; logic and reality of 82; maintenance of 108; Marx's, of production 74, 78, 87; meaning of 43; means for communication in 89–90; mediated by money 88; mediated through culture 59; methods and 49; nature of society and 55; never exist in isolation 46; ongoing process of 154; organisation of 24, 127; persistence of 78; power involved in 79; processes involved in 28; pure modes of 90; real changes in 134; reality of 83, 84; regulation and control of 115; relative independence of 12; reliability in 16; representation of 134; rules for 61; second-order 95, 146; sensate 89; sexuality and 10, 11; society as complex set of 58; state's relation to 116; summed up as risk society 128; third-order 95, 96–7, 139, 145, 146; transformation of ordering of 157; unanticipated consequences of human activities for 159; universal feature underpinning 93; Weber's career devoted to studying 56–7
social transformation 7
social trends 37
social work(ers) 35, 65, 116
socialisation 23

socialism 141, 167; state 92, 158; totalitarian 144; world-wide 158
sociation 81, 90–9
society: animal 49, 90; as country 3; existence of 4, 24, 26, 33, 56–7, 71, 103, 110–12; fluidity of 1, 26, 28, 115, 145; in general 5, 73, 91, 97, 111, 153–4; global society 98; human 1, 2, 5–6, 12–13, 17, 23, 27, 28, 32–5, 38, 46, 49, 70, 73, 85, 90, 96, 99, 102, 129, 130, 146, 149, 163, 165; as nation-state 3–4, 21, 23, 30, 70, 96, 111, 117, 121, 130, 167; in the plural 2, 4, 5, 24, 99; world society 5, 23, 153, 180n27
sociologism 133
sociology: defined 1, 23, 76; French, founder of 22, 126; popularised world-wide 24; science of 31–67; theory 69–105
Socrates 73
solidarity 25, 97
Sorokin, Pitirim 86
Soros, George 82, 162
South Africa 95, 150
sovereignty 118
Soviet Union 3, 4, 22, 64, 120; collapse of 102, 161; see also Chernobyl; Gorbachev; Russia
space 24, 72; 'black holes' in 142; social 51, 91, 129; territorial 51; time and 3, 130, 162; urban 127
specialisation/specialists 92, 108, 110, 124, 160; and reductionism 163–9
specialities 39
Spencer, Herbert 24, 32, 34, 63, 71, 147, 149
sport 97, 114
stability 94, 139
stakeholding 116, 121

Standard Social Science Model 32
standardisation 113
standards 7, 50; academic and professional 54; friendship 59
state benefits 48, 49
state, existence of 151
state societies 114–19; see also city-states; institutions; nation-states
statements 77, 82; baffling 86; controversial 67, 100; universal 58
statistics 35, 40; public 50
status 110, 111, 123–4; occupational 95; ordering of 44, 99; respect for 115; social 14, 35, 58, 121
stereotypes 83, 102
structuration 81, 94–9, 116
structure 72
'struggle for existence' 148
subject matter 52
subordination 8, 92, 111, 144, 150, 156
success 79, 124; economic 123
suicide 77, 126
Sumner, William Graham 34, 65, 73, 109
support 73, 95, 137; moral 63; mutual 44; public 107; victim 144
surveillance 88, 89
surveys 46–7, 50, 51
survival 5, 10, 12, 122; collectivities/institutions 111, 119; non-biological 165; present 145–9
sustainable development 22, 127, 141
symbols 88; shared 44; status 134
systems 88, 111, 147, 155; responsibility 64; rival 167; social 146

Tao 166
taste 117
teams 91

technology 6, 7, 17, 19, 115, 116;
accounts of 79; advance of 88;
dependence on 147; development of
78, 88, 113; history determined by 89;
ideas embodied in 87; imperialist 122;
innovation in 160; new 121, 129, 161;
non-biological survival of 165
television 51
tension 84, 109, 157, 159; creative 168
terms 43, 147; ambiguous 21; discourse
40; identity 102
territory 20, 21
text 50
Thatcher, Margaret (Baroness) 56, 56
theory 33, 38, 45, 49, 69–105; classic 52;
ideology 62; institutional 110–14;
metaphor and 41–3; predictive 38;
psychoanalytic 11
Third Reich see Nazis
'Third Way' 167, 168
Third World 167
thought/thinking 34, 36, 56, 86, 137,
147; Jewish and Muslim 70; radical
119; Western tradition 39
time 24, 86, 146; and space 3, 130, 162
Toffler, Alvin 161
Tönnies, Ferdinand 71, 73, 74
torture 118
Touraine, Alain 76
Toynbee, Arnold 21, 149, 150, 159
trade unions 90, 120, 144
transactions 16, 17
transcendental meditation 156
transformation 5, 7, 23, 120, 124, 137–8;
economic, political and cultural 72;
environmental 128; multiple 130;
social relations 157; world 153
Triads 162
trial and error 112
triangulation 49–52

trust 44, 54, 103–5, 138; naive, in
science 94
truth 14, 32, 49; opposite of 112; simple
quest for 38; universal 59
Turnbull, Colin 122
Tylor, E. B. 131
typifications 83, 102–3
tyranny 118

Uganda (Ik people) 122
uncertainty 103, 112, 144, 160
understanding 32, 33, 37, 42, 51, 82;
acquisition of 113; aids to 83, 147;
common 168; continual updating of
55; core 39; everyday, beyond 53; fact
and values 61; mutual 44; of new
ignorance 152; perfect 86; sociology
for 114; world society as reality 153
unemployment 48, 96; mass 134
unfreedom 81
uniqueness 49, 101; biological 100
United Nations 63, 139, 145
United States 2–3, 4, 12, 34, 37, 53,
151–2; belief in God 137;
communitarian movement 64–5;
control of institutions 116;
corporations 154; creation of new
future 71; media's portrayal of 52;
training in methods of research 66; see
also Carter; Clinton
units 75–7, 82, 100; competition between
148; territorial 129
unity 62
universal statements 58–9; values 58–61,
72
universalism 61; pragmatic 61, 82
universality: of authority 93, 112; of co-
operation and conflict 90; of
ethnocentrism 109; of human problem
146, 147, 161; of human rights 109; o

identity issues 102–3; and ideology 57–61, 77–82; of incest taboo 26; of institutions 139; values 78, 80–2, 140; of work 121
universe 138; expanding 33
urban zoning 128
urbanisation 136
utopia 13, 80, 94; communication 85

value judgements 14
values 6, 7, 56, 76, 80, 98, 121; abstract 137; freedom for 59–62, 166; market 14; new 163; overwhelming influence on 17; prior consensus on 112; religious 14, 137; science and 81; scientific 8; secular 137; sexist 48; shared 89; universal 59; widely used measure of 14
variables 47
Veblen, Thorstein 14, 122, 134
Verwoerd, Hendrik F. 150
Viking literature 129
violence 62, 79, 80, 89, 97; explaining outbreaks of 113; legitimacy of 118; monopoly of 118, 136
virtues 88, 92; civic 135; social 12
voluntaristic theory 76
voting 36, 135, 156

Wales 111
war criminals 118
watching 53
Watson, James D. 38
wealth 9, 14, 15, 82, 162; accounts of very rich on small islands 120; concentration of 16; redistributed 10; untold 155; vast inequalities of 167; voting according to 156
Weber, Max 66, 78, 115, 132, 133, 142; bureaucracy 93; classic definition of nation-state 118; existence of society 56; human reality 61; 'ideal types' 83, 89; individuals 45, 66, 76; Protestant ideas on work 121, 122; religion and capitalism 157; theory of legitimacy 92
welfare 97, 104, 154; statism 120, 147
well-being 70, 168
Williamson, Oliver 140
Willis, Paul 132
Wilson, Edward 6
Wollstonencroft, Mary 10
women 56, 65; and children 123, 124, 130; employment 46–7, 48, 124, 145; rights 10, 62, 146; subordination of 8; violence against 62
work 18, 45, 46–7, 74, 91, 145; for human needs 119–26; incentives to 48; motivation to 111, 123, 124; norms set by workers 109; part-time jobs 48; respect for 115; waged 87
working classes 36, 71, 97, 158
World Congress of Sociology 63
worship 13
Wright Mills, C. 52, 150

xenophobia 23

Zavlaskaya, Tatiana 64
zealots 97
Zen and the Art of Motorcycle Maintenance (Pirsig) 88